ROCKY MOUNTAIN
NATIONAL PARK

Classic Hikes & Climbs

This book is dedicated to my brother, John Roach.
He also reached for the heights.
The following poem left the earth in his memory.

> *Though my soul may set in darkness,*
> *it will rise in perfect light.*
>
> *I have loved the stars too fondly,*
> *to be fearful of the night.*

> —Galileo Galilei (1564–1642)

ROCKY MOUNTAIN NATIONAL PARK

Classic Hikes & Climbs

GERRY ROACH

FULCRUM, INC.
GOLDEN, COLORADO
1988

Copyright © 1988
Fulcrum, Incorporated

Book Design by Chris Bierwirth
Photographs by Gerry Roach

LIBRARY OF CONGRESS
CATALOGING-IN-PUBLICATION DATA

Roach, Gerry
Rocky Mountain National Park: Classic Hikes and Climbs

Includes Index.
1. Rock Climbing—Colorado—
Rocky Mountain National Park—Guide-books.
2. Hiking—Colorado—
Rocky Mountain National Park—Guide-books.
3. Rocky Mountain National Park (Colo.)—Guide-books.
I. Title

GV199.42.C62R627   1988   917.88'69   88-16307
ISBN 1-55591-033-5

Fulcrum, Inc.
Golden, Colorado

Climbing is a dangerous activity. Good decision-making and safe climbing are the responsibility of the individual. This guidebook is not a substitute for sound judgment.

CONTENTS

PHOTOGRAPHS

PREFACE

Rocky Mountain National Park: Classic Hikes and Climbs is a celebration of the joys that come from climbing Colorado's peaks. Rocky Mountain National Park offers the hiker and the mountaineer one of the finest arrays of alpine challenges in the Rocky Mountains. The heart of the park is only a few hours from the Denver metropolitan area. The park's proximity to a major population center makes it even more precious. There is a lifetime of adventures waiting for you in the Colorado mountains!

This guidebook begins with an introductory text, then separates into four sections: trailheads, trails, peaks and routes. Detailed descriptions are included for 21 trailheads, 36 trails, 69 peaks and 141 routes. The guide's scope is from Cameron Pass north of the park to the southern park boundary. Peaks and the routes on them are described from north to south.

I grew up climbing with the following definition of difficulty: 5.7 is HARD climbing, 5.8 is when you are really worried about falling off and 5.9 is when you *are* falling off. If that definition rings a bell, then this book is for you. The hardest climb in this guide is rated 5.6. I have tried to include a mixture of routes that will titillate almost anybody's senses. All of the routes in this guide lead to the summit of a peak.

This guide takes a fresh look at Rocky Mountain National Park. Forty-one percent of the routes are walk-ups (Class 1, Class 2, Easy Snow), 29 percent are scrambles

(Class 3, Moderate Snow) and 30 percent are technical climbs (Class 4, Class 5, Steep Snow). Thirty-two routes have been designated * Classic *. Many of these beautiful routes have never been published before.

This book is designed to be used in conjunction with good maps. The U.S.G.S. quadrangles are recommended. They are available in many shops and at the Map Sales Office in the Denver Federal Center (303-236-7477). The introduction to each chapter specifies which quadrangles are required.

This book describes where to climb but not how to climb. No book can really aid in the process of making judgments. There are several good instructional books that can aid the process of learning fundamentals. For an overall introduction to the sport of mountaineering, I recommend *MOUNTAINEERING, the Freedom of the Hills* by the Seattle Mountaineers. Make sure you get the latest edition of this book, as the earlier editions are badly out of date. In 1987, the fourth edition was the most recent.

Climbing is dangerous, and each individual should approach these great peaks with caution. The routes in this book are described for good summer conditions. Conditions can vary tremendously depending on time of day and time of year. Lightning is always a serious hazard during the summer months in Rocky Mountain National Park.

Conditions on snow climbs can vary from year to year. The amount of snowfall during the winter determines the conditions of many snow climbs in August. Cornices do not form exactly the same way each year. Avalanche conditions in the spring and early summer can be the result of storms that occurred months earlier.

Before charging forth with your city energy and competitive urges, take some time to understand the mountain environment you are about to place yourself in. Carefully study the conditions on your climb. Don't be afraid to back off early in the ascent if the conditions are unfavorable. Better yet, do an easier climb nearby and gain knowledge of the conditions and weather patterns in the area. When conditions are clearly settled, come back and do your dream climb.

This guide is not a history book and does not record the names of the people who did the first ascent of each route. Most of the climbs in this book are easy enough that the first ascent cannot be known with any certainty. These routes belong to everyone.

You can spend days climbing in Colorado and never see another person. Most climbing activity is centered on a handful of routes. If you are tired of crowded routes, then try Cracktop Couloir, the East Face of Nakai, Chaotic Glacier, the Loft Route on Longs or the East Face of Eagles Beak. Colorado is full of wilderness!

Unlike most guidebooks, which are a compilation of many people's route descriptions, this book is the labor of love of one man. I started climbing in Colorado in 1955 and have spent the last 33 years climbing these routes. In 1978, I finished climbing every named peak in Rocky Mountain National Park. I have climbed every peak and 75 percent of the routes in this guide. Many routes were climbed specifically for the preparation of this book, then written up immediately. This guide has been extensively field

checked! I received valuable assistance from Chris Haal-
and, Glen Kaye, Steve Komito, Gary Neptune, Glenn
Porzak and my wife, Deirdre Roach. Precision Visuals
PicSure Plus product was used to create the graphics on the
photographs.

The fact that one person has climbed and reported on
these routes gives consistency to the descriptions. Of
course, errors and inconsistencies may still exist in this
book. For these I can only apologize. I have tried to remain
objective while preparing this guide, but my bias has crept
in from time to time.

This book is not intended to be comprehensive in its
coverage of peaks and routes. It does not reveal all the
secrets of Rocky Mountain National Park. Many more
routes could have been included. For every route I climbed,
I saw two more! Never forget the spirit of discovery. You
should finish each workout, each climb and each book
wanting more.

Anyone who climbs all the classic routes in this guide
deserves the title *Dr. Parkheart*. Anyone who does that plus
climbs all the peaks in Rocky Mountain National Park has
clearly graduated Summit Cum Laude! Climb safely and
don't forget to have fun.

Gerry Roach
May 1988

INTRODUCTION

The mountain splendors of Rocky Mountain National Park need little introduction. Rocky Mountain National Park is one of the most visited parks in the United States. The park contains a total of 124 named peaks above 10,000 feet. Of these, 102 are over 11,000 feet, 79 are over 12,000 feet, 20 are over 13,000 feet and one is over 14,000 feet. These peaks provide one of the finer mountain playgrounds in the country.

Extensive glaciation has carved the north and east faces of the park's peaks into wonderful cirques. These cirques are bristling with excitement. The rock in the park is generally excellent and is far better than that found in other Colorado ranges such as the Elk Range or the San Juans. The alpine nature of the peaks and the excellent rock combine to produce the best concentration of good mountaineering routes in Colorado.

This wonderful park is close to the metropolitan areas of Colorado's Eastern Slope and indeed, any peak in the park can be climbed in one day from the city. Even greater pleasures are available by camping in the park, but this is a controlled activity. A summary of the park regulations for climbing and camping follows.

A permit is NOT required for technical climbing in the park. You are free to climb with abandon, and this is as it should be. Rocky Mountain National Park is one of the most progressive parks in the country for technical climbing. Park officials' landmark decision in 1973 to remove the cables from Longs Peak was ahead of its time. If you think it is difficult to climb in Rocky Mountain National Park, then try Capitol Reef National Park!

The impact of camping on the backcountry is another story, however, and there are regulations controlling all overnight camping in Rocky Mountain National Park. Violators may be issued citations and fined. A written permit is required for any overnight stay in the backcountry. A permit is issued for a designated campsite, a cross-country zone or a bivouac site.

A designated campsite is an established campsite at a fixed location near a maintained trail. Each designated campsite has a name. Campers are limited to three nights at one designated campsite. Parties larger than seven people are not allowed at a single designated campsite.

Cross-country zones are not near maintained trails and can be difficult to reach. Camping is allowed anywhere within a cross-country zone, but camps must be moved at least one mile each night, and no more than two nights can be spent in one zone. Camping is not allowed above treeline, and the upper boundaries of cross-country zones generally follow treeline. Horses, fires and groups larger than seven people are not permitted in cross-country zones.

A camping permit is required for any overnight technical climb and is typically for a bivouac site at the base of a climb. Because a bivouac is intended only as a temporary shelter, a bivouac permit does not allow the use of tents.

Permits can be obtained in advance by mail or in person at the Backcountry Office in Park Headquarters on the east and west sides of the park. Permits are free. Reservation requests can be made by mail or in person at any time of the year. Write the Backcountry Office, Rocky Mountain National Park, Estes Park, Colorado 80517. A map showing all the designated campsites and cross-country zones is available from the Backcountry Office. Information on winter camping, horses, fishing, campsites for the handicapped, technical climbing and bivouacs is also available on request.

Reservation requests are not accepted before January 1st in the year of the trip. Phone reservations are accepted from October through May. Call (303) 586-4459. Backcountry camping is limited to a total of seven nights per person between June and September with an additional 15 nights available between October and May. Permits not picked up by 10 a.m. on the first day of the trip will be cancelled in entirety and given to other backpackers.

In case of emergency, contact a park ranger. You can contact a ranger through Park Headquarters by calling (303) 586-2371 or by having a message relayed through the Estes Park Police Department (911 or 586-4465). Park rangers are responsible for all emergency operations within Rocky Mountain National Park.

Park regulations can seem a bit overwhelming at first, but remember that they are designed to maintain the quality of the park. Preservation of the natural environment is one of the primary charters of the National Park Service. In 1987, I traversed from the southern park boundary to Milner Pass. I spent six consecutive nights in designated campsites and cross-country zones and I only saw only 14 other people! This was an exceptional wilderness experience in one of our most visited national parks. The demand for backcountry camping is high, but all you have to do is plan ahead! Rocky Mountain National Park waits for you.

THE RATING SYSTEM

This guide uses the Yosemite Decimal System to rate the difficulty of each route. The rating for each route has three parts: Grade, Class and Snow Steepness. "Grade" rates the overall difficulty of the route. "Class" rates the most difficult free climbing rock pitch. There are no aid routes in this guide. "Snow Steepness" rates the steepest snow or ice on the route (if any).

Grade

The grade of a route is denoted by a Roman numeral from I to VII, in ascending order of difficulty. This number does NOT apply to individual pitches or moves on the climb. As used in this guide, this number rates the overall length and commitment of a route as follows:

Grade I: A short day climb. May require up to 3,000 vertical feet of elevation gain and/or three pitches of technical climbing.

Grade II: A day climb. May require up to 6,000 vertical feet of elevation gain and/or six pitches of technical climbing.

Grade III: A long day climb. May require up to 10,000 vertical feet of elevation gain and/or 10 pitches of technical climbing.

> **Grade IV:** A very long day climb. Will require MORE THAN 10,000 vertical feet of elevation gain and/or 10 pitches of technical climbing.

The word *Grade* is usually implicit and does not appear in the ratings in this guide. Only the Roman numeral appears. The term *technical climbing* refers to Class 4 or Class 5 climbing on rock, or climbing on a snow slope steeper than 40 degrees. "Classes" are defined below. A "pitch" is usually 100 to 150 feet long.

Any route in this guide can be done in one day from the nearest trailhead. The use of a high camp can make any route easier. The grading in this guide is based on the route being done in one day from the nearest trailhead. If an easy Grade III climb with a lot of elevation gain were done from a high camp, it would only be Grade II or Grade I. To properly grade your ascent from a high camp, evaluate the vertical gain and number of technical pitches from the high camp to the summit(s). As listed above, these two criteria can be used to grade any ascent. There are no Grade IV routes in this guide, but two or more climbs can be combined to produce a route of this grade.

Class

The class of a route is denoted by the word *Class*, followed by a number from 1 to 5.14, in ascending order of difficulty, of the MOST DIFFICULT rock pitch on the route. Difficulties from Class 1 to Class 4 are described with a single digit only. When the difficulty reaches Class 5, the description includes decimal places. Class 5 difficulty ranges from 5.0 to 5.6 in this guide. I have made no attempt to distinguish between 5.0, 5.1 and 5.2. Difficulty in this range is indicated 5.0–5.2.

Adjectives such as *easy, difficult* or *severe* are not used to describe rock pitches. What is easy for one person may be difficult for another, and words like this only confuse the issue. In place of adjectives, examples are used to describe the difficulty of pitches. The answer to the question "Just how hard is Class 3 anyway?" is "Climb the Keyhole Route on Longs Peak, then you will know." A list of example routes follows. The routes are ordered roughly from easiest to hardest within each class.

Class 1:	Flattop Mountain–Flattop Mountain Trail
	Farview Mountain–East Slopes
Class 2:	Copeland Mountain–Northeast Slopes
	Mount Lady Washington–East Slopes
	Storm Peak–East Slopes
Class 3:	Chief Cheley Peak–South Ridge
	Longs Peak–Keyhole
	Mount Meeker–East Ridge (final traverse)
Class 4:	Lead Mountain–North Ridge
	Notchtop Mountain–Southeast Gully and Northwest Ridge
	McHenrys Peak–Arrowhead Arete
Class 5.0–5.2:	Hayden Spire–Southeast Face and Northeast Ridge
	Longs Peak–Notch Couloir

Class 5.3–5.4:	Longs Peak–Kieners
	Little Matterhorn–Southeast Face
	Sharkstooth–East Gully
	Notchtop Mountain–Spiral Route
Class 5.5:	Longs Peak–Keyhole Ridge
Class 5.6:	Spearhead–North Ridge
	Sharkstooth–Northeast Ridge

These difficulty ratings are for good, dry conditions. Remember that rock in the high country can rapidly become more difficult as it becomes wet and that a route can become an entirely different climb when covered with snow. For example, the difficulty of the Keyhole Route on Longs can jump from Class 3 to Class 4 and even Class 5 when it is wet or snow covered.

Descents are not listed for every route in this guide. Summit descents are accomplished by reversing the ascent routes or by descending easier routes. When technical routes are included on a peak, the easiest route is also given and this is usually the logical descent route. There are often several easy routes to choose from. If a peak has no route that is Class 3 or easier, the easiest descent route is discussed. Good mountaineering judgment must be used when selecting descent routes.

Since difficulty on rock is defined by example, people unfamiliar with the Yosemite Decimal System will have to do some climbs before they understand what the different class ratings mean. This is particularly true for the more difficult ratings. For the easier ratings, the following descriptions can help.

Class 1 is trail hiking or any hiking across open country that is no more difficult than walking on a maintained trail. Class 2 is off-trail hiking. In this book, Class 2 typically means bushwhacking or hiking on a talus slope. Handholds are not used for upward movement.

Class 3 is the easiest category of climbing and is sometimes referred to as scrambling. Handholds are looked for and used for upward movement. Basic climbing movements are now in use. Occasionally putting your hand down for balance while crossing a talus slope does not qualify as Class 3. That is still Class 2.

Class 4 and Class 5 are definitely in the realm of climbing. As the difficulty increases, the climbing process becomes more and more thoughtful. For a good understanding of difficulties harder than Class 3, go out and do some of the example climbs.

Snow Steepness

The third part of the rating system used in this guide refers to the STEEPEST snow and/or ice encountered on the route. The Snow Steepness rating is not part of the Yosemite Decimal System and has been added to provide more information about a climb. If there is no snow or ice on a route, then this part of the rating is absent. Since the steepness of a slope can be measured, this part of the rating is easier to define. The following adjectives refer to the angle of a slope.

Easy:	0 to 30 degrees
Moderate:	30 to 45 degrees
Steep:	45 to 60 degrees
Very Steep:	60 to 80 degrees
Vertical:	80 to 90 degrees

Slope angles are seldom measured accurately. The angle is usually determined by the feel of the slope. Even experienced climbers are notorious for guessing a slope angle to be steeper than it really is. I have kept this fact in mind when determining the slope angles used in this guide. When a slope angle is hovering around the critical junction between Moderate and Steep, I have applied the Steep rating.

The difficulty ratings in this book make no statement about the equipment that should or should not be used. They are difficulty ratings pure and simple. Historically, Class 3 meant unroped climbing and Class 4 was roped climbing. Unfortunately, there is a lot of historical momentum behind those old definitions.

Defining difficulty in terms of equipment is baloney. Under the old definition, when people tell me that they "Third Classed" a pitch, all I know is that they climbed it unroped. I do not know how hard it is. After all, the Diamond on Longs Peak (5.10) has been "Third Classed." I know how hard a pitch I am willing to do unroped, but I do not know how hard a pitch THEY are willing to do unroped. We could be at opposite ends of a very wide bell curve!

To get an answer to the question, I find myself nervously eyeing the size of their biceps! Then I realize that bicep size has nothing to do with ability, so I try to peer into their souls to see if they have a death wish. Under the old definition, I need to play God just to figure out how hard a pitch is! There are many individuals who can free solo up and down every route in this guide and many more who cannot do any of the routes, with or without a rope. The decision of when to rope up must always be the individual's.

The Yosemite Decimal System is widely used in this country, but the National Climbing Classification System (NCCS) is also used. The following table summarizes the correspondence between the two systems.

Decimal	NCCS
Class 1	F1
Class 2	F1
Class 3	F2
Class 4	F3
Class 5.0–5.2	F4
Class 5.3–5.4	F5
Class 5.5–5.6	F6
Class 5.7	F7
Class 5.8	F8
Class 5.9	F9
Class 5.10a, b	F10
Class 5.10c, d	F11
Class 5.11a, b	F12
Class 5.11c, d	F13 . . .

PART I

TRAILHEADS AND HIKING TRAILS

The first part of this book gives directions to trailheads and basic information about the main trails of Rocky Mountain National Park. Hiking these trails is a rewarding experience by itself. One of the satisfactions of climbing in Colorado is just getting to the peaks.

The peaks' separation from civilization is what makes them so special. We have plenty of civilization. We need more peaks. A civilized version of a peak is called a gym. There is no comparison between a gym and Longs Peak.

These trails travel through the buffer zone between civilization and the peaks. The approach to a peak is an important transition time when you leave behind the "other world" and prepare yourself for an encounter with the real world.

1 TRAILHEADS

This chapter gives directions to the major trailheads of Rocky Mountain National Park. A trailhead is the important place where the machines of civilization are left behind. The trailhead hears all the hopes, fears and pompous boasting at the beginning of a trip. It also sees all the smiles and frowns at the end of a trip. It hears the victory stories and the horror stories. It feels all the fancy strutting and all the limping, blistered feet. If only the Longs Peak Trailhead could talk. Oh, the stories that it could tell!

Directions to the trailheads begin at a U.S. or Colorado Highway. Colorado 14 between Fort Collins and Walden is north of the park and provides access to trailheads on the north side of the Never Summer Mountains. The major highways leading into Rocky Mountain National Park on the east side of the Continental Divide are U.S. 34 from Loveland and U.S. 36 from Denver and Boulder. These two highways meet at Estes Park just east of the park entrance. U.S. 34 becomes Trail Ridge Road, crosses to the west side of the park and continues past Grand Lake to Granby where it intersects U.S. 40.

This chapter is in two sections: trailheads east of the divide and trailheads west of the divide. Both sections are organized from north to south. Only trailheads that provide access to the peaks in this guide are included.

TRAILHEADS EAST OF THE DIVIDE

Lake Agnes Trailhead

This trailhead is at 10,250 feet and provides access to the Lake Agnes Trail, the Michigan Ditch Trail and the northern end of the Never Summer Mountains. To reach the Lake Agnes Trailhead, go 2.5 miles southwest from Cameron Pass on Colorado 14 or go 7.0 miles east from Gould on Colorado 14. Turn south and go 0.5 miles east on a dirt road to a junction. Turn south (right) and ascend the steep hill for 1.4 miles to the trailhead. This road is passable for most passenger cars.

Michigan Lakes Trailhead

This trailhead is at 9,780 feet and provides access to the Michigan Lakes Trail and the Michigan Ditch Trail. To reach it, go 2.5 miles southwest from Cameron Pass on Colorado 14 or go 7.0 miles east from Gould on Colorado 14. Turn south and go 0.5 miles east on a dirt road to a junction. Continue east (straight) for another 0.6 miles to the trailhead.

La Poudre Pass Trailhead

La Poudre Pass is on the Continental Divide at 10,175 feet and provides access to the east sides of Lulu, Thunder, Neota and the Grand Ditch Trail. It can be reached by vehicle from the east side of the divide but not from the west side.

To reach La Poudre Pass, follow Colorado 14 to Long Draw Road. This turn is 2 miles south of Chambers Lake and 4 miles northeast of Cameron Pass. Follow Long Draw Road for 9 miles to Long Draw Reservoir and continue southwest for another 3.5 miles to La Poudre Pass.

Milner Pass Trailhead

This trailhead is on the Continental Divide at 10,758 feet and provides access to the Ute Trail connecting Milner Pass to Fall River Pass on Trail Ridge Road.

Milner Pass is on U.S. 34 (Trail Ridge Road) 24 miles west of the Beaver Meadows Entrance Station near Rocky Mountain National Park Headquarters on the east side of the divide and 17.3 miles northeast of the Kawuneeche Visitor Center near the west entrance to Rocky Mountain National Park.

Lawn Lake Trailhead

This trailhead is at 8,530 feet and provides access to the Lawn Lake Trail and the Ypsilon Lake Trail. These two trails provide access to the heart of the Mummy Range in Rocky Mountain National Park. Starting at Estes Park, the trailhead can be reached via either U.S. 36 or U.S. 34.

From Rocky Mountain National Park Headquarters on U.S. 36, go west for 1.2 miles to the Beaver Meadows Entrance Station. Continue west on U.S. 36 past the turnoff to Bear Lake. Go 3.1 miles beyond the entrance station to the western junction of U.S. 36 and U.S. 34. Turn north (right) on U.S. 34 and descend north for 1.9 miles to Old Fall River Road. Turn west (left) and go 0.1 miles to the trailhead.

The Lawn Lake Trailhead can also be reached from the eastern junction of U.S. 36 and U.S. 34 on the east side of

Estes Park. Go west on U.S. 34 for 5.1 miles to the Fall River Entrance Station. Continue west on U.S. 34 for another 2.2 miles to Old Fall River Road. Turn west (right) and go 0.1 miles to the trailhead.

Chapin Pass Trailhead

This trailhead is at 11,020 feet and provides access to the Chapin Creek Trail and the west side of the Mummy Range. Refer to the Lawn Lake Trailhead for directions to that point. From the Lawn Lake Trailhead, go west on Old Fall River Road for 8.5 miles to the Chapin Pass Trailhead. Old Fall River Road is one way up. The return from the Chapin Pass Trailhead is via Trail Ridge Road, 2.4 miles west of the trailhead.

Fern Lake Trailhead

This trailhead is at 8,150 feet and provides access to the north end of the Fern Lake Trail. From Rocky Mountain National Park Headquarters on U.S. 36, go west for 1.2 miles to the Beaver Meadows Entrance Station. Continue west on U.S. 36 for another 0.2 miles to Bear Lake Road. Turn south (left) on Bear Lake Road and go 1.3 miles to Moraine Park Road. Turn west (right) on Moraine Park Road and go west for 2.7 miles to the trailhead.

Bear Lake Trailhead

This major trailhead is at 9,450 feet and provides access to the south end of the Fern Lake Trail, the Flattop Mountain Trail, the Dream Lake Trail and the Lake Haiyaha Trail. From Rocky Mountain National Park Headquarters on U.S. 36, go west for 1.2 miles to the Beaver Meadows Entrance Station. Continue west on U.S. 36 for another 0.2 miles to Bear Lake Road. Turn south (left) on Bear Lake Road and go 9.4 miles to the trailhead. There is an enormous parking lot at Bear Lake. Even in summer there is usually no problem parking here before 10 a.m.

Glacier Gorge Trailhead

This trailhead is at 9,240 feet and provides access to the Loch Vale Trail, the Glacier Gorge Trail and the North Longs Peak Trail. From Rocky Mountain National Park Headquarters on U.S. 36, go west for 1.2 miles to the Beaver Meadows Entrance Station. Continue west on U.S. 36 for another 0.2 miles to Bear Lake Road. Turn south (left) on the Bear Lake Road and go 8.6 miles to the trailhead.

There is only one small parking lot at this major trailhead and, on a summer Sunday, it is full by 8 a.m. There is a small overflow parking lot 0.5 miles east of the trailhead, but this is often full as well. Another alternative is to park at Bear Lake and follow a trail southeast for 0.4 miles from Bear Lake to the Glacier Gorge Trailhead. A final alternative is to take the shuttle bus to the trailhead.

Longs Peak Trailhead

This trailhead is at 9,400 feet and provides access to the East Longs Peak Trail. This major trail serves all sides of Longs Peak. The trailhead is west of Colorado 7 and can be reached from either the north or the south.

For the northern approach, measure from the junction of U.S. 36 and Colorado 7, east of Estes Park. Go south on Colorado 7 for 9.2 miles to the turnoff for the Longs Peak Ranger Station. Turn west (right) and go 1 mile to the trailhead.

For the southern approach, measure from the junction of Colorado 7 and Colorado 72 on the Peak to Peak Highway. Go north on Colorado 7 for 10.5 miles to the turnoff for the Longs Peak Ranger Station. Turn west (left) and go 1 mile to the trailhead.

Copeland Lake Trailhead

This trailhead is at 8,350 feet and provides access to the Sandbeach Lake Trail. The south sides of Meeker, Longs and Pagoda can be reached from Sandbeach Lake. The trailhead is west of Colorado 7 and can be reached from either the north or the south.

For the northern approach, measure from the junction of U.S. 36 and Colorado 7 east of Estes Park. Go south on Colorado 7 for 13.1 miles to Wild Basin Road. For the southern approach, measure from the junction of Colorado 7 and Colorado 72 on the Peak to Peak Highway. Go north on Colorado 7 for 6.6 miles to Wild Basin Road.

From the junction of Wild Basin Road and Colorado 7, go west for 0.4 miles on the old highway to another turnoff to Wild Basin and Copeland Lake. Turn west (right) and go 0.1 miles to Copeland Lake and the trailhead. The trail starts on the north side of Copeland Lake and parking is available on the east side of the lake.

Finch Lake Trailhead

This trailhead is at 8,460 feet and provides access to the Finch Lake Trail. Finch Lake can also be reached from the Wild Basin Trailhead, but the hike is 0.7 miles shorter from the Finch Lake Trailhead. Refer to the Copeland Lake Trailhead for directions to Copeland Lake. From Copeland Lake, go west for 1.8 miles to the Finch Lake Trailhead.

Wild Basin Trailhead

This trailhead is at 8,480 feet and provides access to the Lion Lake Trail, the Thunder Lake Trail, the Bluebird Lake Trail and the Finch Lake–Pear Lake Trail. These trails serve all of Wild Basin. Refer to the Copeland Lake Trailhead for directions to Copeland Lake. From Copeland Lake, go west for 2.1 miles to the Wild Basin Trailhead.

Middle Saint Vrain Trailhead

This trailhead is at 8,750 feet and provides access to the Buchanan Pass Trail and the Saint Vrain Glacier Trail. This trailhead is west of Colorado 72 (the Peak to Peak Highway) and it can be reached from the north or the south.

For the northern approach, measure from the junction of Colorado 7 and Colorado 72 on the Peak to Peak Highway. Go south on Colorado 72 for 4.1 miles to Middle Saint Vrain Road. For the southern approach, go north from Ward on Colorado 72 for 6.1 miles to Middle Saint Vrain Road. From the junction of Middle Saint Vrain Road and Colorado 72, go west on Middle Saint Vrain Road for 1.2 miles to the trailhead.

The Buchanan Pass Trail climbs west on the north side

of Middle Saint Vrain Creek and a 4WD road climbs west on the south side of the creek. With a 4WD vehicle you can drive west for an additional 4 miles to the Indian Peaks Wilderness Boundary and reduce the hiking mileage to either Buchanan Pass or the Saint Vrain Glaciers. This road really is a 4WD road and passenger cars will not like it.

TRAILHEADS WEST OF THE DIVIDE

Colorado River Trailhead

This trailhead is at 9,040 feet and provides access to the following trails: the Colorado River Trail, La Poudre Pass Trail, the Thunder Pass Trail, the Red Mountain Trail, the Grand Ditch Trail, the Skeleton Gulch Trail and the Lake of the Clouds Trail. This network of trails serves the east side of the Never Summer Range.

To reach the Colorado River Trailhead, go north 10.1 miles on U.S. 34 from the Kawuneeche Visitor Center near the west entrance of Rocky Mountain National Park. The trailhead is 7.2 miles west of Milner Pass on Trail Ridge Road. The trailhead is marked by signs on the west side of U.S. 34. There is a large parking lot at the trailhead.

Timber Lake Trailhead

This trailhead is at 9,040 feet and provides access to the Timber Lake Trail. To reach the Timber Lake Trailhead, go 10.0 miles north on U.S. 34 from the Kawuneeche Visitor Center near the west entrance of Rocky Mountain National Park. The trailhead is 7.3 miles west of Milner Pass on Trail

Ridge Road. The trailhead is marked by signs on the east side of U.S. 34. There is a large parking lot at the trailhead.

Bowen/Baker Trailhead

This trailhead is at 8,850 feet and provides access to the Baker Gulch Trail and the Bowen Gulch Trail. These trails start in Rocky Mountain National Park but soon cross into Arapaho National Forest and serve the south end of the Never Summer Mountains. To reach the Bowen/Baker Trailhead, go north 6.7 miles on U.S. 34 from the Kawuneeche Visitor Center near the west entrance of Rocky Mountain National Park. The trailhead is 10.6 miles west of Milner Pass on Trail Ridge Road. The trailhead is marked by signs on the west side of U.S. 34. There is a large parking lot at the trailhead.

Onahu Creek Trailhead

This trailhead is at 8,800 feet and provides access to the Onahu Creek Trail. To reach the Onahu Creek Trailhead, go north 3.6 miles on U.S. 34 from the Kawuneeche Visitor Center near the west entrance of Rocky Mountain National Park. The trailhead is 13.7 miles west of Milner Pass on Trail Ridge Road. The trailhead is marked by signs on the west side of U.S. 34. There is a large parking lot at the trailhead.

Green Mountain Trailhead

This trailhead is at 8,800 feet and provides access to the Green Mountain Trail and the Tonahutu Creek Trail. This is the best trailhead to use for destinations in upper Tonahutu Creek. Distances are 2.6 miles shorter than from the Tonahutu/North Inlet Trailhead. To reach the Green Mountain Trailhead, go north 3.0 miles on U.S. 34 from the Kawuneeche Visitor Center near the west entrance of Rocky Mountain National Park. The trailhead is 14.3 miles west of Milner Pass on Trail Ridge Road. The trailhead is marked by signs on the west side U.S. 34. There is a large parking lot at the trailhead.

Tonahutu/North Inlet Trailheads

This trailhead is at 8,500 feet and provides access to the Tonahutu Creek Trail and the North Inlet Trail. If you are destined for upper Tonahutu Creek then this route is 2.6 miles longer than the Green Mountain Trailhead.

To reach the Tonahutu/North Inlet Trailhead, go north three blocks on Garfield Street from the center of Grand Lake to Colorado 278. Go east on Colorado 278 for 0.2 miles, then turn north onto a dirt road. There is a small trailhead sign at this junction. Go north for 0.25 miles to the trailheads near the Grand Lake water treatment plant. There is a small parking lot at the North Inlet Trailhead. When it is full you have to park in Grand Lake or on Colorado 278. It is a 16.3-mile hike to Bear Lake.

East Inlet Trailhead

This trailhead is at 8,400 feet and provides access to the East Inlet Trail. To reach it, go north three blocks on Garfield Street from the center of Grand Lake to Colorado 278. Go east on Colorado 278 for 1.5 miles to the trailhead. Colorado 278 originates on the west side of Grand Lake and provides a direct route from U.S. 34 to the trailhead. It is 2.7 miles from the Grand Lake turn on U.S. 34 to the trailhead. There is a large parking lot at the trailhead.

2 HIKING TRAILS

This chapter describes the major trails of Rocky Mountain National Park. Only the trails that provide access to the peaks in this guide are covered. The minor trails that prowl the lowlands are not included. The intent of this chapter is to provide the basic information required to get you to the high country. Each trail is matched with its parent trailhead(s) and is given a unique name which is used throughout the book.

Sometimes there are multiple names for the same trail. For example, the names used by the National Park Service and U.S. Forest Service do not always match the names on the U.S.G.S. quadrangles. Sometimes the names on signs at the trailheads or along the trail do not match the other sources. In general, I have used the names that appear on the U.S.G.S. quadrangles.

This chapter is in two sections: trails east of the Continental Divide and trails west of the Continental Divide. Both sections are organized from north to south.

TRAILS EAST OF THE DIVIDE

Lake Agnes Trail

This short trail starts at the Lake Agnes Trailhead and climbs south for 0.5 miles to Lake Agnes.

Michigan Lakes Trail

This trail starts at the Michigan Lakes Trailhead, climbs southeast, crosses the Michigan Ditch Trail and continues south and then west to Michigan Lakes at 11,200 feet. From the trailhead, it is 1.5 miles to the Michigan Ditch Trail and 3.5 miles to Michigan Lakes.

The Michigan Lakes have been renamed American Lakes, but they still appear as Michigan Lakes on the 1977 Mount Richthofen Quadrangle. They are referred to as Michigan Lakes in this guide.

Michigan Ditch Trail

This trail is really a road that follows Upper Michigan Ditch between Lake Agnes and Cameron Pass. This is a nearly level hike, as Michigan Ditch drops only 130 vertical feet between Lake Agnes and Cameron Pass. This trail provides an easy route from the Lake Agnes Trailhead to the Michigan Lakes Trail.

The south end of the trail is 0.25 miles south of the Lake Agnes Trailhead and is reached from the Lake Agnes Trail. It can also be reached by bushwhacking straight east for 200 yards from the Lake Agnes Trailhead. From the south end of the Michigan Ditch Trail it is 2.8 miles to the Michigan Lakes Trail and another 2.6 miles to Cameron Pass.

Ute Trail

This trail connects the Milner Pass Trailhead with Fall River Pass on Trail Ridge Road. It provides a nice downhill hike from Fall River Pass at 11,976 feet to Milner Pass at 10,758 feet and is a popular trail in the summer. This Ute Trail should not be confused with another Ute Trail near James Peak.

Starting at the Milner Pass Trailhead, the trail switchbacks up the hill south of the pass before beginning a long ascending traverse to Forest Canyon Pass at 11,300 feet. From this pass, the trail climbs gently northeast to Fall River Pass. It is 2.0 miles from Milner Pass to Forest Canyon Pass and another 2.5 miles to Fall River Pass.

Lawn Lake Trail

This major trail starts at the Lawn Lake Trailhead at 8,530 feet and climbs steadily north for 6.3 miles along the east side of the Roaring River to Lawn Lake at 11,000 feet. The Lawn Lake Trail is joined by the Black Canyon Trail 0.5 miles southeast of Lawn Lake. The Black Canyon Trail climbs for many miles through the depths of Black Canyon southeast of Mummy Mountain and joins the Lawn Lake Trail. A rough, unmaintained trail continues above Lawn Lake to the Saddle between Hagues Peak and Fairchild Mountain at 12,398 feet.

Ypsilon Lake Trail

This trail leaves the Lawn Lake Trail 1.3 miles northwest of the Lawn Lake Trailhead, crosses to the west side of Roaring River and climbs northwest to tiny Chipmunk Lake before descending slightly to Ypsilon Lake at 10,540 feet. The distance from the Lawn Lake Trailhead to Ypsilon Lake is 4.9 miles.

Chapin Creek Trail

This trail starts at the Chapin Pass Trailhead, climbs north for 200 yards to Chapin Pass at 11,150 feet, then goes north down Chapin Creek for 7 miles to the northern park boundary. This trail is maintained for only 0.5 miles past Chapin Pass. Beyond this stretch, hikers have a cross-country route. The Corral Creek Trail runs west from this point for a mile to Long Draw Campground on Long Draw Road south of Colorado 14. The Chapin Creek Trail is faint to nonexistent through the meadows of upper Chapin Creek, but is well marked in the north part of the valley after it is joined by the Poudre River Trail.

Fern Lake Trail

The north end of this trail is at the Fern Lake Trailhead and the south end is at the Bear Lake Trailhead. Between these two trailheads, the trail passes Fern Lake and Odessa Lake and under the Little Matterhorn. It also crosses the saddle between Joe Mills Mountain and Notchtop Mountain near Lake Helene and Two Rivers Lake. Bear Lake is 1,300 vertical feet higher than the Fern Lake Trailhead, so starting at Bear Lake makes an easier one-way hike. This is a very scenic trail.

It is 2.8 miles from Bear Lake to the saddle between Joe Mills Mountain and Notchtop Mountain. It is 4.7 miles from Bear Lake to Fern Lake and another 3.8 miles from Fern Lake to the Fern Lake Trailhead. The total length of the trail is 8.5 miles.

Flattop Mountain Trail

This scenic trail climbs west from the Bear Lake Trailhead and winds up the gentle eastern flank of Flattop Mountain. It is 4.4 miles from Bear Lake to the summit of Flattop Mountain. See the Flattop Mountain Trail Route on Flattop Mountain for more details.

Dream Lake Trail

This trail climbs gently west from the Bear Lake Trailhead to Nymph Lake, Dream Lake and, finally, Emerald Lake underneath Hallett Peak. This is one of the more popular trails in Colorado. It is hiked by thousands of people each summer and for good reason. The distances are short and the adventure quotient is high. From Bear Lake, it is 0.5 miles to Nymph Lake, 1.1 miles to Dream Lake and 1.8 miles to Emerald Lake.

Lake Haiyaha Trail

The north end of this trail leaves the Dream Lake Trail 200 yards east of Dream Lake. The Lake Haiyaha Trail climbs around the east ridge of Hallett Peak to Lake Haiyaha at 10,200 feet in the lower reaches of Chaos Canyon. It is 2.2 miles from Bear Lake to Lake Haiyaha. A rough trail continues south from Lake Haiyaha for another mile to the Loch Vale Trail at 9,800 feet in the saddle between the Glacier Knobs.

Loch Vale Trail

This trail starts at the Glacier Gorge Trailhead, climbs east around the eastern Glacier Knob, then climbs west on the south side of the Glacier Knobs. The trail continues climbing west on the north side of Icy Brook into Loch Vale. Loch Vale is the most intimate valley in Rocky Mountain National Park, and this is one of the most spectacular hikes in Colorado. It is 2.1 miles from the Glacier Gorge Trailhead to the Loch at the entrance to Loch Vale. Beyond here the magic unfolds. The trail continues west for another 1.4 miles to Glass Lake, and finally, Sky Pond at 10,900 feet. The ascent to Glass Lake is rugged and involves a little scrambling.

Variation

There is a good shortcut trail that saves time when hiking from the Glacier Gorge Trailhead to Loch Vale or Glacier Gorge. From the trailhead, follow the Loch Vale Trail for 0.2 miles to the second and larger bridge. The unmarked shortcut trail starts just east of this second bridge on the south (right) side of the main trail. The shortcut trail winds south, traverses west, then climbs south between the Glacier Knobs to rejoin the Loch Vale Trail at 9,780 feet in the saddle between the Glacier Knobs. This upper junction is

100 yards east of the Loch Vale–Glacier Gorge trail junction.

Glacier Gorge Trail

This trail leaves the Loch Vale Trail at 9,800 feet in the saddle between the Glacier Knobs. It crosses to the south side of Icy Brook and climbs south to Mills Lake, then continues south to Black Lake in the heart of Glacier Gorge. It is 2.1 miles from the Glacier Gorge Trailhead to Mills Lake and 4.4 miles from the trailhead to Black Lake. The trail between Mills Lake and Black Lake is rough.

North Longs Peak Trail

This trail leaves the Loch Vale Trail 1.0 miles above the Glacier Gorge Trailhead and climbs southeast for 5.0 miles up vast, open slopes to join the East Longs Peak Trail in Granite Pass at 11,900 feet on the north side of Mount Lady Washington. It is 7.0 miles from the Glacier Gorge Trailhead to the Boulder Field via the North Longs Peak Trail. The North Longs Peak Trail provides a longer but less-crowded alternative to the East Longs Peak Trail.

East Longs Peak Trail

This trail starts at the Longs Peak Trailhead and climbs up the lower, east slopes of Longs Peak and Mount Lady Washington to Mills Moraine. The trail then skirts around the north side of Mount Lady Washington and reaches the Boulder Field on the north side of Longs Peak. This is a very popular trail and is the approach for the Keyhole Route on Longs Peak. Stay left at the Eugenia Mine–Storm Pass junction, left at the Jims Grove junction, right at the Mills Moraine junction and left at the North Longs Peak Trail junction in Granite Pass. It is 5.9 miles from the Longs Peak Trailhead to the Boulder Field.

Sandbeach Lake Trail

This trail starts at the Copeland Lake Trailhead, climbs to the crest of Copeland Moraine, skirts south of Lookout Mountain and crosses Campers Creek and Hunters Creek to reach Sandbeach Lake after 4.0 miles.

Finch Lake Trail

This trail starts at the Finch Lake Trailhead, climbs east then southwest to reach Finch Lake after 4.6 miles. The trail continues west for another 2.0 miles to Pear Lake. This trail is joined after 1.5 miles by the Allenspark–Wild Basin Trail that connects Allenspark to Calypso Cascades on the Wild Basin Trail.

Lion Lake Trail

This trail leaves the Thunder Lake Trail 5.0 miles west of the Wild Basin Trailhead and climbs northwest to Lion Lakes. It is 6.5 miles from the Wild Basin Trailhead to the first Lion Lake. A rough trail continues northwest from the first Lion Lake to the second Lion Lake and Snowbank Lake.

Thunder Lake Trail

This trail starts at the Wild Basin Trailhead and climbs west for 6.8 miles to Thunder Lake in the heart of Wild

Basin. The trail reaches Calypso Cascades after 1.8 miles, where it is joined by the Allenspark–Wild Basin Trail. You can hike east on this trail to reach the Finch Lake Trail. It is 5.3 miles from the Wild Basin Trailhead to Finch Lake via this route. The main Thunder Lake Trail continues west from Calypso Cascades on the south side of North Saint Vrain Creek.

Three hundred yards north of Calypso Cascades, an alternate trail heads west on the north side of North Saint Vrain Creek. There are six designated campsites along this alternate trail, which rejoins the main Thunder Lake Trail at 9,600 feet. This alternate trail misses the junction with the Bluebird Lake Trail, which is 3.3 miles from the trailhead on the main Thunder Lake Trail. The junction with the Lion Lakes Trail is 5.0 miles from the trailhead and 0.7 miles northwest of the point where the alternate trail rejoins the main trail.

Bluebird Lake Trail

This trail leaves the Thunder Lake Trail 3.3 miles west of the Wild Basin Trailhead and climbs west to Bluebird Lake, which is 6.3 miles from the trailhead. A short spur trail also reaches Ouzel Lake, which is 4.9 miles from the Wild Basin Trailhead.

Saint Vrain Glacier Trail

This trail starts from the Buchanan Pass Trail at the Indian Peaks Wilderness boundary on the east side of the Continental Divide. This point is 4 miles west of the Middle Saint Vrain Trailhead. The Saint Vrain Glacier Trail climbs northwest for an additional 4 miles to Gibraltar Lake at the base of the south Saint Vrain Glaciers.

TRAILS WEST OF THE DIVIDE

Thunder Pass Trail

The north end of this trail is at Michigan Lakes and the south end is on the Colorado River Trail 0.25 miles north of Lulu City. From the Colorado River Trail, the Thunder Pass Trail climbs steeply northwest for 1.3 miles between Lulu Creek and Sawmill Creek to Grand Ditch. The trail crosses Grand Ditch on a bridge and climbs north for 1.7 miles across Box Canyon to Thunder Pass at 11,331 feet. Elk spend a lot of time in Box Canyon and can sometimes be seen enjoying the morning sun near Thunder Pass.

Thunder Pass is the northern boundary of Rocky Mountain National Park and from here the trail descends west for 0.5 miles to Michigan Lakes and the Michigan Lakes Trail. The trail crosses a sliver of Routt National Forest between Thunder Pass and Michigan Lakes. Michigan Lakes are in Colorado State Forest. The distance from Lulu City to Michigan Lakes is 3.75 miles and the distance from the Colorado River Trailhead to Michigan Lakes is 7 miles.

La Poudre Pass Trail

The north end of this trail is on the Grand Ditch Trail 1.2 miles southwest of La Poudre Pass, and the south end is on the Colorado River Trail 0.25 miles north of Lulu City.

From the Colorado River Trail, La Poudre Pass Trail climbs northeast for 1.7 miles on the west side of the Colorado River to reach Grand Ditch. The distance from Lulu City to La Poudre Pass is 3.15 miles and the distance from the Colorado River Trailhead to La Poudre Pass is 6.5 miles.

Grand Ditch Trail

This trail is a maintenance road that runs along Grand Ditch on the east side of the Never Summer Mountains. Grand Ditch originates at 10,300 feet in Baker Gulch at the south end of the Never Summer Mountains, runs north along the east side of the range and reaches La Poudre Pass on the Continental Divide at 10,175 feet. The purpose of the ditch is to transfer water from the Western Slope to the Eastern Slope. The length of Grand Ditch is 14.3 miles.

The Grand Ditch Trail provides easy, level hiking along the east side of the Never Summer Mountains. It is reached by La Poudre Pass Trail, the Thunder Pass Trail, the Red Mountain Trail and the Baker Gulch Trail. Bridges cross the ditch at the Thunder Pass Trail, the Skeleton Gulch Trail, the Lake of the Clouds Trail and the Baker Gulch Trail. These bridges are useful since the ditch can be difficult to cross when it is full of water.

Colorado River Trail

This trail starts at the Colorado River Trailhead and goes north along the Colorado River Valley for 3.6 miles to the site of historic Lulu City. The trail continues north for another 0.25 miles to the south ends of the Thunder Pass Trail and La Poudre Pass Trail.

Skeleton Gulch Trail

This trail starts from the Grand Ditch Trail 0.5 miles south of the Grand Ditch–Thunder Pass trail junction. The Skeleton Gulch Trail goes west from Grand Ditch for 1.3 miles to 10,750 feet in Skeleton Gulch.

Lake of the Clouds Trail

This trail starts at the Grand Ditch Trail and climbs west for 1 mile. The last 0.4 miles to Lake of the Clouds at 11,430 feet in upper Hitchens Gulch is rough and not maintained. The Grand Ditch–Lake of the Clouds trail junction is 2.8 miles south of the Grand Ditch–Thunder Pass trail junction and 1.7 miles north of the Grand Ditch–Red Mountain trail junction. The shortest route from the Colorado River Trailhead to Lake of the Clouds is via the Red Mountain Trail.

Red Mountain Trail

This trail starts on the Colorado River Trail 0.5 miles north of the Colorado River Trailhead. The Red Mountain Trail climbs southwest, then north to Grand Ditch. It is 2.2 miles from the Colorado River Trail to Grand Ditch.

Timber Lake Trail

This trail starts at the Timber Lake Trailhead. The trail climbs southeast for 3.2 miles to Long Meadows and continues west to Timber Lake at 11,060 feet on the west side of Mount Ida. It is 4.8 miles from the trailhead to Timber Lake.

Baker Gulch Trail

This trail starts at the Bowen/Baker Trailhead, goes west across the meadows of the Colorado River Valley and enters Arapaho National Forest. The trail then climbs west to Baker Gulch and Grand Ditch. The trail crosses Grand Ditch on a bridge and climbs north through upper Baker Gulch to Baker Pass at 11,253 feet. It is 3.7 miles from the trailhead to Grand Ditch and another 2.5 miles to Baker Pass. A spur trail leaves the Baker Gulch Trail 0.3 miles north of Grand Ditch and climbs west for 1.2 miles to Parika Lake at 11,380 feet.

Bowen Gulch Trail

This trail starts at the Bowen/Baker Trailhead, goes west across the meadows of the Colorado River Valley and enters Arapaho National Forest. The trail goes south to Bowen Gulch, climbs west into Bowen Gulch, and finally climbs north to Bowen Pass at 11,476 feet. It is 8.2 miles from the trailhead to Bowen Pass. A spur trail leaves the Bowen Gulch Trail at 10,400 feet and climbs south for 1.2 miles to Bowen Lake at 11,019 feet.

Onahu Creek Trail

This trail starts at the Onahu Creek Trailhead and goes northeast for 2.5 miles to a trail junction in Onahu Creek. The Timber Creek Trail goes north from here for 3.2 miles through Long Meadows to the Timber Lake Trail at 10,640 feet. The Onahu Creek Trail continues south for another 1.5 miles to the Tonahutu Creek Trail at the north end of Big Meadows. A nice 7.4 mile hike can be done from the Onahu

Creek Trailhead to the Green Mountain Trailhead via the Onahu Creek Trail, the Tonahutu Creek Trail and the Green Mountain Trail.

Green Mountain Trail

This short trail starts at the Green Mountain Trailhead and goes east for 1.8 miles to the Tonahutu Creek Trail on the west side of Big Meadows. This trail is useful as a shortcut to the Tonahutu Creek Trail. It is 11.6 miles from the Green Mountain Trailhead to Flattop Mountain and 14.2 miles from the Tonahutu/North Inlet Trailhead to Flattop Mountain. The Green Mountain Trail saves 2.6 miles when hiking to Flattop Mountain via the Tonahutu Creek Trail.

Tonahutu Creek Trail

This major trail starts at the Tonahutu/North Inlet Trailhead and ends on top of Flattop Mountain. From the trailhead, the trail goes north for 4.4 miles to Big Meadows. From the north end of Big Meadows, the trail climbs east up Tonahutu Creek to treeline then climbs southeast above treeline to Flattop Mountain. The trail meets the North Inlet Trail and the Flattop Mountain Trail on Flattop Mountain. The Tonahutu Creek Trail is very popular in the summer for trans-Continental Divide hikes. It is 14.2 miles from the trailhead to Flattop Mountain.

North Inlet Trail

This major trail starts at the Tonahutu/North Inlet Trailhead and ends on top of Flattop Mountain. From the trailhead, the trail goes east through Summerland Park and continues climbing northeast then east up the North Inlet valley. The trail leaves the North Inlet at 9,600 feet and climbs east into Hallett Creek to treeline. The trail switchbacks above treeline, then climbs lazily north to Flattop Mountain. A maintained spur trail leaves the North Inlet Trail at 9,600 feet and climbs south to Lake Nokoni and Lake Nanita.

It is 12.8 miles from the trailhead to Flattop Mountain and 9.9 miles from the trailhead to Lake Nokoni. It is 16.3 miles to Bear Lake via the North Inlet Trail.

East Inlet Trail

This trail starts at the East Inlet Trailhead and climbs east up the East Inlet valley. The trail is quite good to Lake Verna but is not maintained east of Spirit Lake. A faint trail climbs to Boulder–Grand Pass from the north side of Fourth Lake. It is 5.5 miles to Lone Pine Lake, 6.9 miles to Lake Verna, 7.5 miles to Spirit Lake and 9.0 miles to Boulder–Grand Pass.

Variation

The unmaintained Paradise Park Trail leaves the East Inlet Trail 100 feet east of the bridge across the East Inlet Creek at 9,400 feet. This junction is 1 mile west of Lone Pine Lake. The East Inlet–Paradise Park Trail junction is deliberately not marked. The Paradise Park Trail goes south for 1 mile then slowly dies into the wilderness of this magic place. Camping is not permitted in Paradise Park, but day hiking is allowed.

PART II

THE PEAKS

There's torment in the wind today,
It screams with anguish on its way;
And something in its frenzied cry
Resounds within me in reply:

Oh frantic wind—I know! I know!
And I will join you as you go—
Escaping dread, unseen distress,
We'll leap into the wilderness,
And whirl this fright and fury out,
And whip away all clinging doubt;
Then softly glide back in the night—
Released and calmed by our wild flight.

—Eloise Roach©

3 NEVER SUMMER MOUNTAINS

The Never Summer Mountains extend from Cameron Pass in the north to a point west of Bowen Pass in the south. The Never Summer Mountains are 15 miles long, and most of the peaks in this small range are on the Continental Divide. The Continental Divide does a big S turn through the Never Summer Mountains and actually runs "backwards." In other words, the divide's north-south journey through the state goes south-north for 15 miles. If that isn't confusing enough, the Eastern Slope is on the west and the Western Slope is on the east! Fortunately, your compass will still point north. Just don't turn the map upside down!

The Continental Divide through the Never Summer Mountains is the western boundary of Rocky Mountain National Park. Approaches from the east are in the park, approaches from the north are in Colorado State Forest and approaches from the south are in either Routt or Arapaho national forests. The following trailheads serve the Never Summer Mountains: Lake Agnes, Michigan Lakes, La Poudre Pass, Colorado River and Bowen/Baker. The following U.S.G.S. quadrangles cover this area: Mount Richthofen, Fall River Pass, Bowen Mountain and Grand Lake.

For mountaineers, the salient feature of the Never Summer Mountains is the bad rock. This range is out of character with the rest of Rocky Mountain National Park. The Never Summer Mountains are pretty to look at, but on a closer inspection, its perverse nature is revealed. Many climbers have found themselves poised on disintegrating, volcanic slopes with emotions ranging from disgust to terror. There are very few good mountaineering routes in the Never Summer Mountains. The easier summits provide pleasant hikes.

NOKHU CRAGS 12,485 feet

Nokhu Crags are prominent from near the top of Cameron Pass on Colorado 14. They form the northernmost rampart of the Never Summer Mountains. Their alluring name, distant location and craggy nature entice mountaineers with the promise of a special adventure. Although Nokhu Crags are visually appealing, the dream fades as soon as the rotten rock of this area is encountered. Climbers who have experienced the solid classics farther south need to approach Nokhu Crags with care. In spite of the rotten rock, these exciting and difficult summits attract mountaineers. Climbers often ascend them in winter when the rock is covered with snow and, hopefully, frozen in place.

Nokhu Crags consist of a northern and a southern summit. The northern summit is slightly higher and more difficult than the southern summit. It is not reasonable to traverse between the two summits, so the choice of which summit to ascend must be made early. The ridge between the two summits contains some large, rotten cliffs and is not recommended. For the routes on these summits, use the Lake Agnes and Michigan Lakes trailheads. Nokhu Crags are in Colorado State Forest just outside the park.

Northern Summit–North Face I, Class 4

This is the easiest route to the northern summit of Nokhu Crags. It is also the descent route from the northern summit. It approaches the peak up the north ridge of the northern summit, then winds up through a series of gullies on the north face of the peak. Finding the easiest way through the network of gullies requires good route-finding skills. There is a lot of loose rock in these gullies, and this is not a good route for a large party.

From the Lake Agnes Trailhead, bushwhack east for 200 yards to the Michigan Ditch Trail. Follow this trail north for 0.8 miles. Avoid the temptation to leave the ditch and cut up to the north ridge of the northern summit too soon. The west-facing slopes below this ridge are steep and miserable. From a suitable spot directly north of the summit, leave Michigan Ditch and climb south up the north ridge to a small point at 12,200 feet. The summit is now looming dramatically overhead.

From the small point, do not continue directly up the ridge above. It is festooned with rotten gendarmes and can lead you into a lot of trouble. Descend on the west side of the ridge for 300 feet to avoid the west ridge of the first gendarme. When it is easy to continue south toward the peak, do an ascending traverse on ledges and scree slopes to a tiny bowl northwest of the final summit cliffs.

The exact route from this point to the summit is difficult to describe, and careful route-finding is required. There are some false cairns on the route.

From the tiny bowl, climb south up a broad, scree-filled alleyway. Do not continue up the obvious, steep gully to the south. Turn east (left) and head up a narrowing, steepening gully. Do not follow this gully all the way to the north ridge. Leave the gully, turn south (right) and scramble south up a 15-foot-wide gully. This small gully is the logical and physical crux of the route. It requires some careful Class 4 climbing, as loose rocks abound. From the upper end of the gully, the summit is a short Class 3 scramble southeast.

Grand Central Couloir II, Class 4, Steep Snow

This couloir is on the east side of Nokhu Crags and reaches the notch between the northern and southern summits. It is the premier mountaineering route on Nokhu Crags, but should be attempted only when conditions are favorable. When avalanche conditions are stable, it can provide a good winter climb. During May and June it is usually snow filled. By July, the bottom half of the couloir melts out and leaves a grubby, rubble-filled gully. This couloir is not easily seen. The best distant vantage point is Iron Mountain.

The east side of the crags can be approached from either the Lake Agnes Trailhead or the Michigan Lakes Trailhead. From the Lake Agnes Trailhead, bushwhack east for 200 yards to the Michigan Ditch Trail. Follow this trail north and east for 1.5 miles as it swings around the north ridge of the northern summit. Once you are east of this ridge, leave Michigan Ditch and bushwhack southwest for 1 mile into the upper basin underneath the east face of the northern summit. Grand Central Couloir is not visible until you are nearly at the base of it.

From the Michigan Lakes Trailhead, follow the Michigan Lakes Trail for 3.5 miles to Michigan Lakes. From the easternmost lake, contour at 11,300 feet around the ridge north of the lake. Once you are on the north side of this ridge, descend west to 11,000 feet, then climb west for 0.4 miles into the upper basin.

The couloir is 500 feet high, and the climb varies depending on conditions. Rockfall from the northern summit can be a problem, and a helmet is recommended. The angle is not uniform and there are some steep bulges in the upper part of the couloir. From the notch between the summits, the southern summit is a 300-foot, Class 4 climb. It is not reasonable to reach the northern summit from this notch. Descend via Nokhuloir to return to Michigan Lakes or via the Southern Summit–West Face Route to return to Lake Agnes.

Nokhuloir I, Class 3, Moderate Snow

This couloir is on the east side of Nokhu Crags and reaches the saddle just south of the southern summit. Grand Central Couloir and Nokhuloir bind the east face of the southern summit. Nokhuloir is a broader, lower-angled and friendlier couloir than Grand Central Couloir. When snow conditions are favorable, it provides the easiest route up the southern summit. Like Grand Central Couloir, Nokhuloir is difficult to see until you are well up into the basin below the east face. Nokhuloir is in good condition in June. The lower part of Nokhuloir melts out by July, leaving a section of scree.

Follow one of the approaches described for Grand Central Couloir and, from the bowels of the basin, stay south (left) of the southern summit to enter Nokhuloir. The couloir is 550 feet high and the steepest snow is near the top. The couloir ends at a small saddle south of the southern summit at 12,340+ feet. The southern summit is a short Class 3 scramble north from this saddle. Descend by reversing the Nokhuloir or descending the Southern Summit–West Face Route.

Extra Credit

From the southern summit, scramble south and ascend the North Ridge Route on Static Peak. From Static, you can continue south to Richthofen and descend the West Ridge Route on that peak to Lake Agnes. From Static, you can also descend the East Ridge Route to Michigan Lakes. Either alternative provides a nice circle tour and extends the adventure.

Southern Summit-West Face I, Class 3

This route provides access to the southern summit from Lake Agnes. From the Lake Agnes Trailhead, follow the Lake Agnes Trail for 0.5 miles to Lake Agnes, hike around the west side of the lake and continue south for a few hundred yards beyond the south end of the lake. Turn east (left) and consider your future. A steep, 1,000-foot scree slope leads up to the south ridge of the southern summit. Scrabble up this miserable slope. Once you are on the ridge, head north over Point 12,440+ feet, and scramble north to the southern summit (Class 3).

THUNDER MOUNTAIN	12,040+ feet
LULU MOUNTAIN	12,228 feet
MOUNT NEOTA	11,734 feet

These easy peaks are on the Continental Divide 2 miles east of Michigan Lakes and Nokhu Crags. They are outliers of the Never Summer Mountains and are easily climbed together. The rock on these peaks is not good. The peaks can be approached from either the Michigan Lakes Trailhead or La Poudre Pass Trailhead.

West Ridge I, Class 2

From the Michigan Lakes Trailhead, follow the Michigan Lakes Trail for 3.5 miles to Michigan Lakes and continue southeast on the Thunder Pass Trail for another 0.5 miles to 11,331-foot Thunder Pass on the Continental Divide. From Thunder Pass, ascend the west ridge of Lulu and traverse northeast for 0.6 miles to Thunder. If you are inspired, descend southeast for another 0.5 miles to the uninspired summit of Neota. Return to the Thunder–Lulu saddle and descend northwest on steep scree back to the Michigan Lakes Trail.

East Ridge I, Class 2

This route starts at La Poudre Pass Trailhead, which is the best starting place if you want to ascend all three of these summits together. From La Poudre Pass, climb northwest for 1.3 miles to the summit of Neota and continue northwest for another 0.5 miles to Thunder. Traverse southwest for 0.6 miles to the summit of Lulu. Descend southeast for 0.7 miles from Lulu to Point 11,739 feet. Descend east from Point 11,739 feet for 1.1 miles to Bennett Creek above Grand Ditch and hike northeast for 0.5 miles back to La Poudre Pass.

STATIC PEAK 12,560+ feet

This elegant peak is on the Continental Divide 0.6 miles south of Nokhu Crags and 0.5 miles north of Mount Richthofen. Static has three ridges and three faces. The ridges provide interesting routes, but the faces are to be avoided as the rock is not good. Static can be approached from either the Lake Agnes Trailhead or the Michigan Lakes Trailhead. The choice of trailhead depends on the route.

North Ridge I, Class 5.0–5.2

This is the most difficult of Static's three ridges. It provides a short, airy tour. This ridge is used when climbing the southern Nokhu Crag and Static together. This climb can be approached from either the Lake Agnes Trailhead or the Michigan Lakes Trailhead. From the Lake Agnes Trailhead, follow the Southern Summit–West Face Route on Nokhu Crags to the 12,140-foot saddle between the southern summit of Nokhu Crags and Static.

From the Michigan Lakes Trailhead, follow the Michigan Lakes Trail for 3.5 miles to Michigan Lakes and continue west to Snow Lake at 11,516 feet. From the west end of Snow Lake, climb west for 0.2 miles to the 12,140-foot saddle between the southern summit of Nokhu Crags and Static. This face is quite broken and, with careful route-finding, the difficulty does not exceed Class 4.

From the saddle, turn south and climb 0.25 miles to the summit. Stay on the west side of the ridge. In the center of the ridge, there are some short sections requiring 5.0–5.2 climbing.

East Ridge I, Class 3

This ridge is inspiring to look at and fun to climb. If you are looking for a knife edge, this is it! The upper part of the ridge is a true east ridge, but the lower part of the ridge faces north and rises above the east end of Snow Lake. Approach this climb from the Michigan Lakes Trailhead. Follow the Michigan Lakes Trail for 3.5 miles to Michigan Lakes and continue west to Snow Lake at 11,516 feet.

From the east end of Snow Lake, climb south and get onto the broad, lower portion of the ridge. This section of the ridge is broken and can be ascended with Class 2 hiking up to 12,200 feet. From here, turn west and consider your future. The final 0.25 miles along the upper east ridge require some serious Class-3 scrambling along a very exposed knife edge. The rock is not solid, and great care should be used on this ridge. In spite of the bad rock, this ridge provides the joys of scrambling along a high, exposed ridge to a spectacular summit.

Extra Credit

From Michigan Lakes, hike south to the Continental Divide and climb Point 12,018 feet, alias "The Electrode."

Both the east and west ridges of "The Electrode" are Class 2 hikes. This is a significant summit which rises at least 298 vertical feet above its connecting saddle with Static. From the summit of "The Electrode" there is a good end-on view of the east ridge of Static and a good view of the broken east face of Mount Richthofen.

South Ridge II, Class 2

This is the easiest route to the summit of Static and also the ridge to use when climbing Static and Richthofen together. Start by making an ascent of Richthofen. Static is 0.5 miles north of Richthofen. The traverse between the two peaks is a Class 2 hike on scree.

The easiest descent back to Lake Agnes is to reverse the route and climb back over the top of Richthofen. Be sure to allow time for the return trip. The second ascent of Richthofen makes this climb a Grade II. Re-ascending Richthofen is tougher than climbing Static in the first place!

MOUNT RICHTHOFEN 12,940 feet

Mount Richthofen is the highest peak in the Never Summer Mountains and the undisputed monarch of the area. It is on the Continental Divide 1 mile southeast of Lake Agnes. Richthofen just misses 13,000 feet but is still Colorado's highest peak on the divide north of Milner Pass. Richthofen is the most sought-after summit in the Never Summer Mountains and provides a refreshing outing.

West Ridge I, Class 2

This is the easiest and most-used route on Richthofen. From the Lake Agnes Trailhead, follow the Lake Agnes Trail south for 0.5 miles to Lake Agnes. Hike around the west side of the lake and continue south for another mile to the 12,000-foot saddle west of Richthofen. The slopes below the saddle contain easy snow in June, which is easier to climb than the scree that appears later in the summer.

From the saddle, climb east up the broad west ridge for 0.25 miles to a shoulder at 12,800 feet and continue east for 270 yards to the summit. The scree slope between the saddle and the shoulder is a bit steep, but there are no technical difficulties. Never has there been such a summer summit!

Extra Credit

From the 12,000-foot saddle, climb west for 0.4 miles to the 12,493-foot summit of "Mahler Peak." This is a significant summit that rises almost 500 vertical feet above the saddle connecting it to Richthofen. "Mahler Peak" is quite prominent from Lake Agnes.

The east ridge of "Mahler Peak" is broken and rotten, so a direct ascent along the ridge is not reasonable. Stay below the ridge crest on the south side of the ridge and scramble in and out of rotten, Class 4 gullies as you work your way west. Mahler will be pleased that you have worked so hard for so little!

The easiest way to reach the Lake Agnes Trailhead from the summit of "Mahler Peak" is to descend west and then north for 0.7 miles to Point 11,960+ feet. From here, descend north for 0.8 miles to the trailhead. Your Tour de

Mahler is complete!

TEPEE MOUNTAIN 12,360+ feet

This small, curious peak is on the Continental Divide 0.5 miles south of Mount Richthofen. Tepee has eastern and western summits. The western summit is slightly higher. Tepee has steep southeast and north faces and the blunt east ridge between these faces is often seen in profile from vantage points to the south. Tepee is usually climbed together with Mount Richthofen.

North Ridge II, Class 2

This is the easiest route on Tepee and begins with an ascent of Mount Richthofen. From the summit of Richthofen, descend west for 270 yards to a shoulder at 12,800 feet. From here, descend the south ridge of Richthofen and ascend the short north ridge of Tepee. The traverse between Richthofen and Tepee is a rough hike on scree. Be prepared for a little scrambling along the way. The easiest return to Lake Agnes is to reverse the route.

North Face Couloir II, Class 3, Steep Snow

This north-facing couloir reaches the notch between Tepee's eastern and western summits. It provides a good early-summer snow climb, but after the snow melts out, this couloir is to be avoided. Because the approach to the couloir is long, this climb can be greatly aided by a high camp.

See Lead Mountain for directions to 10,800 feet in upper Skeleton Gulch. From here, climb northwest for 0.7

miles into the upper basin between Richthofen and Tepee.
The couloir is not visible until this high basin is reached.
The couloir rises 500 vertical feet in the center of Tepee's
small north face. The steepest portion is short. The rock
here is rotten, and a helmet is recommended for this climb.
From the notch between the summits, scramble west to the
highest point.

The easiest descent back into Skeleton Gulch is to
descend Tepee's south ridge for 0.35 miles to the 11,930-
foot saddle between Tepee and Lead. From this saddle,
descend east into Skeleton Gulch. The slopes just below the
saddle are steep and require some scrambling.

LEAD MOUNTAIN 12,537 feet

This peak is on the Continental Divide 1 mile south of
Tepee Mountain and 1 mile north of Mount Cirrus. There
is a ridge running east from Lead Mountain that separates
Skeleton Gulch to the north from Hitchens Gulch to the
south. Lead can be approached from either of these gulches.

To reach Skeleton Gulch, start at the Colorado River
Trailhead and follow the Colorado River Trail north for 3.6
miles to Lulu City. From here, follow the Thunder Pass
Trail northwest for another 1.5 miles to Grand Ditch.
Follow Grand Ditch south for 0.5 miles to Sawmill Creek
and follow the Skeleton Gulch Trail west for 1.3 miles to
10,750 feet in upper Skeleton Gulch.

To reach Hitchens Gulch, start at the Colorado River
Trailhead and follow the Colorado River Trail north for 0.5

miles to its junction with the Red Mountain Trail. Follow the Red Mountain Trail west for 2.2 miles to Grand Ditch and follow Grand Ditch north for 1.7 miles to Hitchens Gulch. Cross the ditch and follow the Lake of the Clouds Trail west for 1.2 miles to 11,000 feet in Hitchens Gulch. To approach Lead, it is not necessary to go all the way to Lake of the Clouds.

North Ridge II, Class 4

This ridge is most often used when climbing Tepee and Lead together, but it can also be reached from upper Skeleton Gulch. The crux of the ridge is above the 11,930-foot saddle between Tepee and Lead. The steep east face below the ridge discourages any climbing on that side of the ridge. The crest of the ridge is exposed and undesirable. The west side of the ridge is also steep, but offers the path of least resistance.

From the 11,930-foot saddle between Tepee and Lead, hike south for 200 yards. From here, stay well below the ridge crest on the west side of the ridge, traverse south across 250 yards of Class 4 slabs and climb south to Point 12,200+ feet. From here, hike south along the narrow ridge for 0.4 miles to the summit. To descend to Skeleton Gulch or Hitchens Gulch, use the East Ridge Route.

East Ridge II, Class 2, Easy Snow

This is a good, early-summer climb when snow covers the scree. From 10,800 feet in upper Skeleton Gulch, climb south for 0.7 miles to the 12,000-foot saddle east of Lead. In June, there is a long, easy snow slope below the saddle, which greatly facilitates progress. This saddle can also be reached from Hitchens Gulch via a steep scree slope. From the saddle, climb west for .3 miles up the enjoyable east ridge to the summit.

Extra Credit

From the 12,000-foot saddle east of Lead, climb east for 0.25 miles to Point 12,438 feet. This is a significant summit, which rises at least 438 vertical feet from its connecting saddle to Lead.

MOUNT CIRRUS 12,797 feet

This mountain is on the Continental Divide 1 mile south of Lead Mountain. It is at the head of Hitchens Gulch. The peak has a pretty name but does not excite much mountaineering interest. An ascent of Cirrus does allow you to visit beautiful Lake of the Clouds.

South Slopes II, Class 2

See Lead Mountain for directions to 11,000 feet in Hitchens Gulch. Continue southwest to Lake of the Clouds at 11,430 feet. From here, climb west for 0.5 miles to the 12,400-foot saddle south of Cirrus. The slopes below the saddle are steep scree, but there are no technical difficulties. From the saddle, walk north up the gentle south slopes of Cirrus for 0.3 miles to the summit.

HOWARD MOUNTAIN 12,810 feet

This peak is on the Continental Divide 0.6 miles south of Mount Cirrus and 0.5 miles southwest of Lake of the Clouds, at the head of Hitchens Gulch. Howard Mountain is the second highest peak in the Never Summer Mountains, but it provides little mountaineering interest.

Northwest Ridge II, Class 2
Follow the South Slopes Route on Mount Cirrus to the 12,400-foot saddle between Cirrus and Howard. Hike southeast for 0.4 miles to the summit of Howard.

East Ridge II, Class 3
Follow the South Slopes Route on Mount Cirrus to Lake of the Clouds. From the east side of Lake of the Clouds, scramble south up a steep, broken slope to Point 12,440+ feet. From here, scramble west along the gentle east ridge of Howard for 0.6 miles to the summit.

MOUNT CUMULUS 12,725 feet

This peak is on the Continental Divide 1.2 miles south of Howard Mountain and 0.8 miles northeast of Baker Pass. Mount Cumulus is the archetypal Never Summer peak. It is a great heap of scree! Its name is more exciting than its slopes.

East Slopes II, Class 2

This is the shortest route on Cumulus. Start at the Colorado River Trailhead and follow the Colorado River Trail north for 0.5 miles to its junction with the Red Mountain Trail. Follow the Red Mountain Trail west for 2.2 miles to Grand Ditch and follow Grand Ditch west for 0.6 miles to Mosquito Creek. Bushwhack west for 0.7 miles to treeline, pick a route up onto the broad east ridge of Cumulus and follow it west for a final mile to the summit. You are now well on your way to the Master of Scree Degree!

MOUNT NIMBUS	**12,706 feet,**
MOUNT STRATUS	**12,520+ feet**
BAKER MOUNTAIN	**12,397 feet**

These three peaks are not on the Continental Divide. The divide swings west to Baker Pass, and these peaks are southern outliers of the long Never Summer ridge. These three peaks are usually climbed together.

West Slopes II, Class 2

Any or all of these peaks can be climbed from the west via the Baker Gulch Trail. From the Bowen/Baker Trailhead, follow the Baker Gulch Trail west for 4.0 miles to a junction at 10,400 feet with a spur trail that leads west to Parika Lake. Continue north on the Baker Gulch Trail toward Baker Pass.

Any of the summits can be reached by scrambling up

the steep, west-facing scree slope east of the trail. The best itinerary for climbing all three peaks is to continue north on the Baker Gulch Trail all the way to Baker Pass and climb east up steep scree to Mount Nimbus. Traverse south for 0.4 miles to Mount Stratus and continue south for another 0.6 miles to Baker Mountain. Descend west from Baker down steep scree and return to the Baker Gulch Trail.

PARIKA PEAK 12,394 feet
FARVIEW MOUNTAIN 12,246 feet

These two gentle peaks are on the Continental Divide 2.2 miles southwest of Baker Pass. They are easily approached via good trails and are usually climbed together. They make a nice day climb.

East Slopes II, Class 1

From the Bowen/Baker Trailhead, follow the Baker Gulch Trail west for 4.0 miles to a junction at 10,400 feet with a spur trail. Follow this spur trail west for 1.2 miles to Parika Lake at 11,400 feet. From Parika Lake, continue west on a trail to the 12,000-foot saddle between Parika and Farview. Farview is 300 yards south of the saddle and Parika is 0.4 miles north of the saddle. The highest point of Parika is 200 yards northwest of the Continental Divide.

Extra Credit

From either Parika Lake or Parika Peak, go to the 11,700-foot saddle east of Parika Peak. Climb east for 0.3

miles to Point 12,253 feet, alias "Paprika Peak." This is a significant summit that rises at least 533 vertical feet above its connecting saddle to Parika Peak. Many named peaks do not have that much relief from their highest saddle connecting them to higher ground.

BOWEN MOUNTAIN 12,524 feet

The summit of Bowen is 0.5 miles southeast of the Continental Divide on a ridge extending east from the divide. This ridge separates Baker Gulch to the north from Bowen Gulch to the south. Bowen Mountain is the highest peak south of Baker Pass in the Never Summer Mountains. The faces of Bowen are steep and the rock is rotten. The routes on this peak follow the ridges.

Northeast Ridge II, Class 3

This is the easiest route on Bowen. The approach to the northeast ridge of Bowen can be made from either Baker Gulch or Bowen Gulch. To approach via Baker Gulch, start at the Bowen/Baker Trailhead and follow the Baker Gulch Trail west for 3.7 miles to Grand Ditch at 10,300 feet. Leave the Baker Gulch Trail and follow Grand Ditch southwest for 0.3 miles. Leave the ditch and bushwhack southwest for 0.4 miles to treeline in the basin north of Bowen Mountain. From here, climb west for 0.7 miles to reach the Continental Divide at 12,200 feet between Point 12,442 feet, alias "Never Summer Peak," and Point 12,280+ feet. Climb south for 0.2 miles to the summit of Point 12,280+ feet.

The approach via Bowen Gulch is easier but 3.3 miles longer than the approach from Baker Gulch. From the Bowen/Baker Trailhead, follow the Bowen Gulch Trail for 8.2 miles to Bowen Pass at 11,476 feet on the Continental Divide. From Bowen Pass, climb east for 0.4 miles to Point 12,280+ feet.

From Point 12,280+ feet, climb southeast for 0.5 miles along Bowens northeast ridge to the summit. The ridge is rotten, but any gendarmes can be easily bypassed. Some Class 3 scrambling is required.

Extra Credit

From Point 12,280+ feet, climb north for 0.4 miles to Point 12,442 feet, alias "Never Summer Peak." This is a fun little peak with an impressive north face.

East Ridge II, Class 4

This is the shortest route up Bowen. Follow the Baker Gulch approach on the Northeast Ridge Route to treeline in the basin north of Bowen. From here, pick a suitable route and climb south to reach the east ridge of Bowen near 12,000 feet (Class 3).

Scramble west across some small points (Class 3) to the bottom of a steep, rotten headwall at 12,120 feet. This headwall can be ascended directly with 120 feet of Class 4 climbing on very rotten rock, or it can be bypassed to the south. Bypassing the headwall involves traversing on steep, hard-packed dirt slopes (Class 3). This headwall is a nasty obstacle which makes this an undesirable route. Above the headwall, 100 yards of Class 3 scrambling lead up to the summit. Descend one of the other routes.

South Ridge II, Class 3

This is the shortest route up Bowen Mountain when approaching on the Bowen Gulch Trail. From the Bowen/ Baker Trailhead, follow the Bowen Gulch Trail for 5.4 miles to 9,700 feet. Leave the trail and bushwhack north for 0.7 miles to Blue Lake at 10,690 feet. From Blue Lake, climb west on a curving ridge for 0.5 miles to Point 12,084 feet and hike north along Bowen Mountain's south ridge for 0.6 miles to the summit.

4 MUMMY RANGE

The Mummy Range is a collection of peaks in northern Rocky Mountain National Park that is completely independent of the Continental Divide. The range is between Trail Ridge Road and the northern park boundary. The Mummys contain a surprising seven peaks over 13,000 feet, which is more than a third of the thirteeners in the park. Hagues Peak, at 13,560 feet, is the highest peak in the Mummys and the fourth highest peak in the park.

The peaks in the Mummy Range are high, but generally easy to climb. There is a walk-up route on every peak. The southeast face of Ypsilon is the dramatic exception to the otherwise gentle terrain. This great cirque contains the best mountaineering routes in the Mummys. The Mummy Range is approached from the Lawn Lake Trailhead and the Chapin Pass Trailhead. The following U.S.G.S. quadrangles cover this area: Trail Ridge Road and Estes Park.

HAGUES PEAK 13,560 feet

Hagues is the highest peak in the Mummy Range, the highest peak in Larimer County and the fourth highest peak in Rocky Mountain National Park. It sits in the middle of the Mummy Range, 1.5 miles northwest of Lawn Lake. Hagues is not the most prominent peak in the Mummy Range, as it is often obscured by other peaks. When viewed from the south, it has a long, flat east ridge and a short, steep west ridge. Hagues is easy to climb and provides a good introduction to the Mummy Range.

West Ridge II, Class 2

This is the standard route up Hagues, and the main difficulty is the 5,000 vertical feet that must be gained from the trailhead. Start at the Lawn Lake Trailhead and follow the Lawn Lake Trail north for 6.3 miles to Lawn Lake at 10,900 feet.

Lawn Lake is best known for the time its dam broke and the water from the lake roared down through Estes Park. The scars from this flood still remain. Prophetically, the creek below the lake is named Roaring River! A high camp can aid this long climb. There are designated campsites along the Roaring River and at Lawn Lake.

From Lawn Lake, continue northwest on a rough trail for another 2 miles to the 12,398-foot saddle between Hagues Peak and Fairchild Mountain. This saddle carries the uninspired name *the Saddle*. From the Saddle, climb northeast on talus for 0.7 miles on the south side of Hagues' west ridge to the summit.

Extra Credit

From the summit of Hagues, descend north, skirt east of the small Rowe Glacier and climb Rowe Peak (13,400+ feet). Continue north for another 0.5 miles across easy talus to the humble summit of Rowe Mountain (13,184 feet). For people who are trying to climb every thirteener in Rocky Mountain National Park, this is a required assignment. Some spice can be added to the task by ascending the Rowe Glacier directly to the summit of Rowe Peak.

MUMMY MOUNTAIN 13,425 feet

This peak is 1.4 miles southeast of Hagues. Mummy has a rugged southwest face rising directly above Lawn Lake, while its other slopes are expansive and gentle. Hagues and Mummy are often climbed together.

North Slopes II, Class 2
Follow Hagues' West Ridge Route to the summit of Hagues. From here, hike east for 0.7 miles to Point 13,302 feet and then hike southeast for another 0.8 miles to the summit of Mummy. There are no technical difficulties on this traverse. Descend via Mummy's South Slopes Route.

South Slopes II, Class 2
This is the shortest route to the summit of Mummy and the best route for a one-day ascent. From the Lawn Lake Trailhead, follow the Lawn Lake Trail north for 5.8 miles to 10,830 feet and the junction with the Black Canyon Trail. Follow the Black Canyon Trail southeast for 0.3 miles to its high point at 11,100 feet, leave the trail and hike north up the talus-covered south slopes of Mummy for 1.2 miles to the summit.

FAIRCHILD MOUNTAIN 13,502 feet

This rounded mountain is 1.5 miles southwest of Hagues. Fairchild has a small, steep east face above Crystal Lake which excites some technical passions. For the hiker, an ascent of Fairchild can allow the gentle spirit of the mountains to flow freely. Unfettered by strife and striving, you can be lost in time on Fairchild.

Northeast Slopes II, Class 2

Follow Hagues' West Ridge Route to 12,000-feet elevation south of the Saddle. It is not necessary to go all the way to the Saddle at 12,398 feet, but this extra excursion only makes the hike a little longer. From 12,000 feet, hike southwest up talus for 0.9 miles to the summit. Take your time or, better yet, let time take you for once.

YPSILON MOUNTAIN 13,514 feet

Ypsilon is 3.7 miles southwest of Hagues, the fifth highest peak in Rocky Mountain National Park and the second highest peak in the Mummy Range. The west side of the peak is gentle and the east side isn't there! A great void fills the volume that should be Ypsilon's east side. A large, concave southeast-facing cirque embraces this void. The cirque is easily seen and it is marked by the pronounced Y Couloir, which gives Ypsilon its name.

Ypsilon is the home of the best mountaineering routes in the Mummy Range, and its faces offer a wide variety of routes. The southeastern cirque of Ypsilon is approached from the Lawn Lake Trailhead. Follow the Lawn Lake Trail for 1.3 miles to its junction with the Ypsilon Lake Trail. Follow the Ypsilon Lake Trail northwest for another 3.6 miles to Ypsilon Lake at 10,500 feet. There is a designated campsite near Chipmunk Lake. A high camp can greatly aid an ascent on the east side of Ypsilon.

Southwest Slopes I, Class 2

This is the easiest and shortest route to the summit of Ypsilon. It offers the hiker an easy tour to a high summit with spectacular views down into the southeastern cirque. From the Chapin Pass Trailhead, follow the Chapin Creek Trail for 200 yards to Chapin Pass. There is a short spur trail leading east from Chapin Pass. From Chapin Pass, hike east for 0.75 miles, then northeast for 2.2 miles across broad, open slopes to the summit.

Donner Ridge II, Class 3

Donner Ridge is the southeast ridge of Ypsilon and forms the southern boundary of the great southeastern cirque. This is the easiest route up Ypsilon Mountain from Ypsilon Lake and the best route for a direct descent to Ypsilon Lake. From Ypsilon Lake, hike west for 1 mile to 12,000 feet in the basin between Ypsilon and Chiquita.

The Donner Ridge Route does not ascend the broken crest of the ridge directly. From 12,000 feet, climb north up a broken south face that is west of the ridge to reach easy ground at 13,200 feet. Climbing encounters on this face are Class 3. From 13,200 feet, the summit is 0.3 miles north.

Y Couloir III, Class 5.3–5.4, Steep Snow * Classic *

This is the premier mountaineering route in the Mummy Range. Y Couloir is the prominent couloir in the middle of Ypsilon's large southeast face. It provides 1,900 vertical feet of snow climbing. There are two branches to Y Couloir, and either branch provides an exciting climb. Poised on steep snow in the center of a major mountain cirque, you can feel supreme.

Y Couloir has been popular over the years because of its easy visibility, but just because a climb is popular is no reason to approach it casually. Conditions should be studied carefully before attempting either branch. In early June, the couloir is prone to avalanching. Large cornices threaten both branches of the couloir until well into July. These cornices have broken off in mid-summer and produced some epic accidents. It is prudent to avoid Y Couloir until mid-July.

From Ypsilon Lake, hike west for 0.2 miles, then steeply north for 0.3 miles to eastern Spectacle Lake. The two Spectacle Lakes lie in the basin below the great southeastern cirque of Ypsilon. This is indeed a spectacular place. Continue west on the south sides of both Spectacle Lakes and consider your future. Y Couloir starts 250 yards above western Spectacle Lake.

Y Couloir is a single couloir for the first 700 vertical feet and the angle here is moderate. The couloir branches at 12,300 feet and the decision of which couloir to ascend must be made. The southern (left) branch is easier, while the northern (right) branch goes more directly to the summit.

The southern (left) branch is continuous snow, reaches

50 degrees at 12,700 feet and is shorter than the northern branch. The major problem with the southern branch is the cornice at the top. The top of the couloir is wide and the angle can reach 60 degrees as the cornice is approached. You can avoid the cornice by climbing the rocks south (left) of the couloir (5.0–5.2). From the top of the southern branch, the summit is 250 yards north.

The major problem with the northern (right) branch is that it is not continuous snow. There is a 200-foot gap in the snow at 12,600 feet that is almost always present. Climb two 5.3–5.4 rock pitches on the west (left) side of the couloir to bypass the gap. Above the gap, get back into the couloir and follow it steeply toward the summit.

The snow in the upper part of the northern branch is continuous 50 degrees. An uncontrolled fall from this position would catapult you off the top of the gap into another life. This is a bad visualization, but it can happen. Concentrate on the next step and make it a good one!

The snow steepens as the summit approaches and any cornice can be avoided by climbing a 100-foot, Class 4 pitch up the rocks on the east (right) side of the couloir. The northern branch of Y Couloir provides the most direct finish in the Mummy Range. You will know Y as you emerge from the couloir. Be careful that you don't stumble over the summit cairn!

Variation

When conditions permit, the gap in the northern branch of Y Couloir can be climbed directly. In heavy snow years, a nearly vertical snow and ice hose forms in the back of the gap. Climb a long pitch up the ice hose to a platform below a 10-foot chockstone at the top of the gap. Stem around the west (left) side of the chockstone (5.6) to reach the upper part of the couloir.

Blitzen Ridge III, Class 5.4–5.6

Blitzen Ridge is the east ridge of Ypsilon Mountain. It forms the north edge of the great cirque and starts right above Ypsilon Lake. The ridge is punctuated by four gendarmes, which are northeast of western Spectacle Lake. These gendarmes are known as the Four Aces, and passing them is the crux of the route. This is a long climb but the difficult sections are short. The difficulty on this climb can vary considerably depending on the exact route chosen.

Hike 300 yards north from the east end of Ypsilon Lake to 11,100 feet, get on the broad lower portion of the ridge and hike northwest for 0.6 miles to Point 12,044 feet. Continue northwest along the very narrow ridge to the Four Aces. The first three Aces can be bypassed on the north (right) side of the ridge (Class 4) or climbed directly (5.0–5.3).

Getting around the fourth Ace is harder, and this is the crux of the route. Traverse north and then climb west to the notch on the west side of the fourth Ace (5.4–5.6). There are many ways to execute this maneuver. After you pass the fourth Ace, climb west on a Class 3 ridge for 0.3 miles to the summit.

MOUNT CHIQUITA 13,069 feet

This peak is 1 mile southwest of Ypsilon Mountain and is an echo of that great peak. It has the same configuration as Ypsilon, but all the faces are on a smaller scale. It is a good place for peak baggers to play, but does not excite much technical interest. Mount Chiquita carries the distinction of being the lowest thirteener in Rocky Mountain National Park. Remember that good experiences often occur on small peaks.

Southwest Slopes I, Class 2

This is the easiest and shortest route to the summit of Chiquita. In fact, this route is the easiest way to climb a thirteener in Rocky Mountain National Park. From the Chapin Pass Trailhead, follow the Chapin Creek Trail for 200 yards to Chapin Pass. There is a short spur trail leading east from Chapin Pass. From Chapin Pass, hike east for 0.75 miles, then northeast for 1.6 miles across broad, open slopes to the summit.

Extra Credit

Either going to or returning from the summit of Chiquita, take the time to visit the summit of Mount Chapin (12,454 feet). Mount Chapin is 1.4 miles east of Chapin Pass and is only a small addition to the direct route up Chiquita.

East Ridge II, Class 2

This is the easiest way to climb Chiquita from the

vicinity of Ypsilon Lake. From the Lawn Lake Trailhead, follow the Lawn Lake Trail for 1.3 miles to its junction with the Ypsilon Lake Trail. Follow the Ypsilon Lake Trail northwest for another 3.1 miles to tiny Chipmunk Lake at 10,660 feet. It is not necessary to go all the way to Ypsilon Lake.

Leave the trail and bushwhack west for 0.7 miles to Point 12,005 feet on the east end of Chiquita's east ridge. From here, follow the easy, gentle ridge west for 0.6 miles to Point 12,537 feet, then climb northwest for 0.4 miles up talus to the rounded summit.

5 La Poudre Pass to Sprague Pass

This chapter covers the peaks on or east of the Continental Divide between La Poudre Pass and Sprague Pass. La Poudre Pass is on the park boundary in the northwest part of the park. This pass is at the northern end of the Continental Divide's big S turn through the Never Summer Mountains. Sprague Pass is at the west end of Spruce Canyon, which is the first major drainage north of the Bear Lake area. Milner Pass is between La Poudre Pass and Sprague Pass. Milner Pass is where Trail Ridge Road crosses the Continental Divide.

South of Milner Pass, the peaks become more interesting and there are some very remote summits on this section of the divide. The peaks between La Poudre Pass and Sprague Pass are not as exciting as the great peaks farther south, but they do offer some excellent mountaineering routes and true isolation from other wilderness travelers. The following U.S.G.S. quadrangles cover this area: Fall River Pass, Trail Ridge Road, Grand Lake and McHenrys Peak.

SPECIMEN MOUNTAIN 12,489 feet

This peak is on the Continental Divide 2.5 miles southeast of La Poudre Pass and 1.7 miles north of Milner Pass. It is the only named peak between these two passes. Its summit is permanently closed year-round to protect its population of bighorn sheep.

MOUNT IDA 12,880+ feet

This gentle peak is on the Continental Divide 4 miles south of Milner Pass on Trail Ridge Road. Ida is the first named summit south of Milner Pass. This peak is where the action starts, and Ida is a favorite goal for hikers.

North Ridge I, Class 2

This hike may seem long to the uninitiated, but it is gentle. The hike is 10 miles round-trip but the elevation gain is only 2,130 feet. The hardest part is reaching treeline. From the Milner Pass Trailhead, start out on the Ute Trail, which connects Milner Pass and Fall River Pass. Hike on this trail for 0.8 miles as it switchbacks up the north-facing slope. Find a spur trail leading steeply up the hill to the south. This unmarked and unmaintained trail leaves the Ute Trail in the middle of a long ascending traverse at 11,100 feet. This point is still below treeline.

Follow the spur trail as it climbs around to the west side of Point 11,881 feet and passes treeline. Once you reach treeline, it is easy to hike up onto the crest of the Continental Divide south of Point 11,881 feet. The spur trail slowly degenerates into a maze of game trails on the west side of the divide, but is useful for a mile beyond treeline.

Hike south along the divide to Point 12,150 feet and continue south for another 2 miles to the summit of Mount

Ida. Much of this hike is on grassy slopes which become rockier as the summit is approached.

West Slopes II, Class 2

This route up Ida is longer and requires more elevation gain than the North Ridge Route. This route is most often used from a camp in the Timber Creek drainage. From the Timber Lake Trailhead, follow the Timber Lake Trail for 4.8 miles to Timber Lake at 11,060 feet. From the south side of Timber Lake, hike south, then southeast for 0.5 miles to the 11,740-foot saddle between Mount Ida and Point 11,880+ feet. From the saddle, climb east up gentle slopes for 0.7 miles to the summit.

CHIEF CHELEY PEAK 12,804 feet

This peak is on the Continental Divide 0.4 miles southeast of Mount Ida. Chief Cheley Peak is the home of the Iron Men of Haiyaha but don't worry, it is an easy peak to climb. Chief Cheley is usually climbed together with Mount Ida.

Northwest Ridge II, Class 2

Follow one of the routes to the summit of Mount Ida. Descend the southeast side of Ida (Class 2) to the 12,350-foot saddle between Ida and Chief Cheley. The southeast slope of Ida is steep near the summit and a little route-finding is required to find the easiest route. From the Ida–Chief Cheley saddle, climb southeast up the talus slopes on the west side of Chief Cheley's northwest ridge to the summit.

South Ridge II, Class 3

The Continental Divide south of Chief Cheley is a Class 2 hike for many miles. The south ridge of Chief Cheley is used on traverses of the divide or in combination with other peaks to the south. Use any of the routes that lead to the divide south of Chief Cheley. The final approach to the summit of Chief Cheley from the south is along a narrow, exposed ridge that requires a little Class 3 scrambling.

CRACKTOP 12,760+ feet

The summit of this peak is 270 yards east of the Continental Divide and 0.8 miles southeast of Mount Ida. Cracktop is usually climbed together with some of the other peaks in the area. The name *Cracktop* derives from a distinctive, northeast-facing couloir that splits the steep east face of this peak. Cracktop Couloir is easily visible from the high point on Trail Ridge Road.

West Ridge II, Class 3

This is the easiest route to the summit of Cracktop. It can be approached by descending the South Ridge of Chief Cheley or by walking north along the Continental Divide from Sprague Mountain. Hike east and descend slightly to a small saddle 150 yards west of Cracktop's summit. The final ridge requires some minimal Class 3 scrambling.

Cracktop Couloir III, Class 3, Steep Snow * Classic *

This route ascends the namesake couloir splitting Cracktop's east face. Snow remains in the middle part of this couloir through August, but the top part melts out as summer progresses. This climb is in the best condition in late June or early July. When the snow is in good condition, this is a magnificent climb.

There are two approaches to the start of the climb, and they are both long. The first approach starts at either Milner Pass or the Fall River Pass on Trail Ridge Road. Either route leads to Forest Canyon Pass. From Forest Canyon Pass, do a 3.5-mile traverse southeast across rolling country on the east side of the Continental Divide to reach Arrowhead Lake. From Arrowhead Lake, continue south for another mile past Inkwell Lake and reach the bottom of the couloir at 11,700 feet.

The second approach starts with an ascent of Mount Ida. Descend to the saddle between Ida and Chief Cheley, then descend east to Azure Lake at 11,900 feet. This descent involves some moderate snow in June and July. From Azure Lake, contour southeast for 0.4 miles, descending slightly, to reach the bottom of the couloir.

The couloir is deeply inset into the face and a helmet is recommended for this route. Moderate snow leads up to 12,000 feet where the couloir turns west (right) and steepens abruptly. The angle of the upper couloir varies between 50 and 60 degrees for 700 vertical feet. The couloir finishes steeply but without a cornice in a small notch between Cracktop's two small summits. The higher summit is 100 feet west.

TERRA TOMAH MOUNTAIN 12,718 feet

This wonderful mountain is 1.4 miles northeast of the Continental Divide at the end of a ridge that projects into Forest Canyon. This ridge also contains Cracktop and Mount Julian. Terra Tomah is a large, round mountain with steep slopes and a gentle summit. Terra Tomah is easily seen across Forest Canyon from the Forest Canyon Overlook on Trail Ridge Road.

Once, a hardy soul decided to train for an ascent of Longs Peak by climbing the relatively low summit of Terra Tomah. After both Terra Tomah and Longs had been ascended, Terra Tomah was declared the harder peak to climb! Even though this peak looks benign from Trail Ridge Road, the trailless abyss of Forest Canyon stands between the road and the peak. Terra Tomah is a wilderness peak and, in my opinion, one of the most alluring peaks in Rocky Mountain National Park. No other peak offers such a sense of wilderness so close to a road.

Northwest Ridge II, Class 3

This is the shortest and easiest route on Terra Tomah. Start at the Forest Canyon Overlook on Trail Ridge Road. The peak is only 2.4 miles away from this point, but hold on to your hat! The challenge is met immediately. Descend southwest from the overlook for almost 2,000 vertical feet into Forest Canyon. This descent is steep and time consuming but does not require more than an occasional bit of Class 3 scrambling.

Cross to the south side of Big Thompson River near

9,800 feet. This river crossing can be difficult and dangerous during June or July. Occasionally, a large log falls
across the river and produces a natural bridge. All you have
to do is find one.

Once you are on the south side of the river, bushwhack
southwest up to Forest Lake at 10,298 feet. From Forest
Lake, climb west then south to reach the short, stubby
northwest ridge of Terra Tomah at 11,350 feet. Hike west
over Point 11,643 feet and continue southwest up the crux
of the ridge. The crux is a steep, 400-foot-high section in the
ridge and requires some Class 3 scrambling. Climbing this
crux seems like a rite of passage to the wilderness. Once you
are above this crux, the slope angle moderates rapidly and
the highest point of Terra Tomah is another 0.5 miles southwest.

MOUNT JULIAN 12,928 feet

Mount Julian is 0.75 miles northeast of the Continental
Divide on a long ridge that also contains the summits of
Cracktop and Terra Tomah Mountain. If Julian reached the
elevation of 13,000 feet, it would receive more attention
but, as it is, it rests in splendid isolation. It is easily seen
from Trail Ridge Road but is seldom climbed. When it is
climbed, it is usually combined with Cracktop and/or Terra
Tomah.

Southwest Ridge II, Class 3

This is the ridge that connects Mount Julian with

Cracktop. Start by making an ascent of Cracktop. From the summit of Cracktop, descend east on the narrow and exposed ridge to the Cracktop-Julian saddle (Class 3). From the saddle, ascend northeast up talus slopes to the summit of Julian (Class 2).

Northeast Ridge II, Class 2

This is the ridge that connects Julian with Terra Tomah. Start by making an ascent of the Northeast Ridge Route on Terra Tomah. That is the hardest part. Julian is 0.6 miles southwest of Terra Tomah, and the traverse between these two peaks is a gentle walk.

HAYDEN SPIRE 12,480+ feet

This peak is at the head of Hayden Gorge 0.5 miles northwest of Sprague Mountain. The summit of Hayden Spire is the high point of a ridge running northeast from the Continental Divide. Hayden Spire is not a large peak, but it is steep and beautiful. There is actually a series of spires in upper Hayden Gorge, and the lower spires northeast of Hayden Spire have steep east faces. Hayden Spire is easily seen from Trail Ridge Road across the great gulf of Forest Canyon, but it is one of the hardest peaks to reach in Rocky Mountain National Park. It is a test piece for serious peak baggers.

There are two approaches to Hayden Spire. The first approach is from the Continental Divide. Either follow one of the routes up Sprague Mountain and continue northwest on

Southeast Face and Northeast Ridge of Hayden Spire. August 15, 1987.
The northeast ridge is right of the summit.

the divide for another 0.3 miles, or hike southeast along the divide for 8 miles from Milner Pass.

The second approach reaches the peak via Hayden Gorge. To do this, descend southwest from the Forest Canyon Overlook on Trail Ridge Road for 2,100 vertical feet and cross Forest Canyon. The river crossing in the canyon can be difficult in June and July. Continue south and bushwhack for 2.5 miles up Hayden Gorge to the base of the lower spires. Stay below the east faces of these spires and continue south for another 0.5 miles to Lonesome Lake.

Hayden Spire is difficult to climb in one day, but it can be done. A rugged, rewarding Tour de Hayden Spire is to approach via Hayden Gorge, climb the spire, then climb up to the Continental Divide and hike to Milner Pass.

Descent

Descend the Southeast Face and Northeast Ridge Route.

Southeast Face and Northeast Ridge II, Class 5.0–5.2 * Classic *

This is the easiest route on Hayden Spire. The start of the climb differs depending on the approach used. The initial goal is to reach a point on the northeast ridge of Hayden Spire between Hayden Spire and the 12,320+ feet summit of the lower spire, which is 0.2 miles northeast of Hayden Spire.

From Lonesome Lake, hike northwest up a long scree slope to reach the northeast ridge. From the Continental Divide, do a long descending traverse across the southeast face of Hayden Spire (Class 4). Some route-finding is required to find the easiest set of ledges. Avoid the temptation to cut up too soon. There is one couloir that looks tempting, but it runs into more difficult climbing higher up. Traverse all the way around, descending if necessary, to reach easier ground near the northeast ridge.

Once you are on the northeast ridge, ascend it to the summit. The crux pitch is near the summit and requires some 5.0–5.2 climbing up to, and then through, a hole. Above the hole, Class 3 scrambling leads to the summit.

SPRAGUE MOUNTAIN 12,713 feet

This remote peak is on the Continental Divide between Spruce Canyon to the east and Tonahutu Creek to the west. It is 0.9 miles north of Sprague Pass. Sprague Mountain can be seen from Trail Ridge Road, but is overshadowed by the huge mass of Stones Peak, which lies 1 mile to the northeast. Sprague is easy to climb, but the approaches to it are long. Sprague is often climbed by people doing the Milner Pass to Bear Lake Divide Traverse. See the Special Events chapter for details on this traverse.

South Slopes II, Class 2

This is the easiest route up Sprague and is just a long hike. It is a Grade I day hike from a camp in upper Tonahutu Creek. From the Green Mountain Trailhead on the west side of the divide, follow the Green Mountain Trail east for 1.8 miles to Big Meadows and the Tonahutu Creek Trail.

Follow the Tonahutu Creek Trail north, then east for another 5.7 miles to a point just above treeline at 11,100 feet. Leave the Tonahutu Creek Trail and climb north up a steep grass slope. There is an old, unmaintained trail near here that heads for Sprague Pass. It is not necessary to go to Sprague Pass, but this trail can be used for awhile to get up the steep part of the slope.

Sprague Pass can also be reached from Bear Lake on the east side of the divide. Hike 4.4 miles to the summit of Flattop Mountain on the Flattop Mountain Trail and descend northwest for 2.3 miles on the upper part of the Tonahutu Creek Trail. Leave the Tonahutu Creek Trail at 11,800 feet and hike north for another 0.8 miles to Sprague Pass.

The distance to Sprague Pass is the same from the east or the west. Once you are in the vicinity of Sprague Pass, continue north up the rounding slope for a long mile to the flat summit of Sprague Mountain.

Sprague Glacier II, Class 3, Steep Snow/Ice

Sprague Glacier is on the east side of the Continental Divide 0.5 miles southeast of Sprague Mountain. This glacier is difficult to reach and it is seldom climbed. If you can get there, it provides a unique and steep climb in a wilderness setting. The upper part of the glacier turns to ice in August.

Sprague Glacier from the north. Rainbow Lake is on the left. August 15, 1987.

There are two ways to approach the bottom of this glacier. The first approach route is an 8-mile hike with some difficult bushwhacking. Start at either Bear Lake or the Fern Lake Trailhead and follow the Fern Lake Trail to a point 200 yards north of Fern Lake. From here, hike 0.6 miles northwest to Spruce Lake on a trail and then contour around to the north side of Castle Rock and get into Spruce Canyon. Bushwhack west up Spruce Canyon for 2 miles to Rainbow Lake and the base of the glacier.

The second approach route is an 8.5-mile hike that avoids the bushwhacking but requires more elevation gain. Follow the South Slopes Route and continue to Sprague Pass. From Sprague Pass, contour north at 11,800 feet, then descend northeast until you can climb northwest to Rainbow Lake and the base of the glacier.

The glacier provides 500 vertical feet of steepening snow and ice. It reaches a maximum angle of 60 degrees near the top, where there may be a small cornice. The glacier reaches the divide at 12,360 feet and the summit of Sprague Mountain is 0.5 miles northwest.

STONES PEAK 12,922 feet

Stones Peak forms a large massif that projects northeast of Sprague Mountain and the Continental Divide. The summit of Stones is 1 mile northeast of Sprague Mountain. A lower, unnamed peak ("Stapps," 12,736 feet) is 0.6 miles northeast of Stones. The massif is bounded by Hayden Gorge to the northwest, Forest Canyon to the northeast and

Spruce Canyon to the south. All three of these wild valleys are trailless, allowing Stones Peak to reside in isolated splendor.

Stones and the unnamed summit are connected by a broad, easy ridge and they are usually climbed together. Stones is easily seen across Forest Canyon from Trail Ridge Road. Ascending both Stones and the unnamed peak is simply a long walk. Getting there is the major problem.

Southwest Ridge II, Class 2

Follow one of the routes to the summit of Sprague Mountain. Stones is reached from the summit of Sprague by hiking along the connecting ridge between these two peaks.

Southeast Slopes II, Class 2

This is the shortest route to the summit of Stones. Start on the Spruce Canyon approach for the Sprague Glacier Route on Sprague Mountain. From Spruce Lake, bushwhack north and cross Spruce Canyon at 9,500 feet. Ascend the long southeast ridge of the unnamed peak and continue southwest to Stones.

6 BEAR LAKE AREA

This chapter covers the peaks on or east of the Continental Divide from Sprague Pass to Andrews Pass. All of these peaks can be approached from Bear Lake. These are some of the more accessible peaks in the park and they are also some of the best. There are many excellent routes within a few miles of Bear Lake. Most of the routes are Grade I. There are no Grade III climbs in this chapter. The following U.S.G.S. quadrangle covers this area: McHenrys Peak.

Bear Lake is in the center of the park, and this area is truly the heart of the park. There are a wide variety of rock routes, snow routes and walk-up routes to choose from on the slopes of these peaks. A lifetime of adventure begins here.

LITTLE MATTERHORN 11,586 feet

Little Matterhorn is 0.5 miles west of the Continental Divide and 0.6 miles north of the more famous Notchtop Mountain. The summit of Little Matterhorn is just at the end of a ridge extending east from Knobtop Mountain. Little Matterhorn gets its stature from its steep east and north faces. The peak is spectacular when viewed from Lake Odessa and has some fun routes. Little Matterhorn also has the distinction of being the lowest peak in this book.

Little Matterhorn is easily approached. Refer to Notch-top Mountain for the approach to Lake Helene. From the northwest side of Lake Helene, follow an old trail down to Grace Falls. From here, climb north to reach the south side of the peak.

Southeast Face I, Class 5.3–5.5

Climbing on this face is largely a matter of choice, and some general directions are given to aid this process. The steep lower buttress can be avoided by climbing up 5.0–5.2 slabs west (left) of it. The upper buttress contains two or three pitches of good 5.3–5.5 climbing which lead you naturally onto the exposed crest of a southeast ridge as the summit is approached.

Southwest Face I, Class 3

This is the easiest route on Little Matterhorn. It sneaks around the cliffs and approaches the summit from the west. From the south side of the peak, hike to the west of all the cliffs and ascend north up a scree slope. Do not go all the way up to the ridge. Stay on the south side of the ridge and do an ascending traverse east across steep scree toward the summit. Reach the ridge 200 yards west of the summit and scramble east along it (Class 3) to the summit, which consists of a very small rise near the end of the ridge.

Extra Credit

From the start of the ascending traverse, climb west to Knobtop Mountain (Class 3).

NOTCHTOP MOUNTAIN 12,129 feet

The humble height of this peak is overshadowed by its soaring cliffs. Notchtop is 0.2 miles east of the Continental Divide and 2.5 miles northwest of Bear Lake. The peak is not visible from Bear Lake, as it is hidden by the large mass of Flattop Mountain 0.7 miles to the south. The summit of Notchtop is a spire standing above 800-foot-high north, east and south faces. The namesake notch is 100 feet deep and is west of the summit. The peak is connected to the Continental Divide by its jagged northwest ridge.

Notchtop is impressive when viewed from the Fern Lake Trail near Two Rivers Lake and Lake Helene. The rock on this peak is generally solid and offers some tantalizing routes. There are several technical rock climbs on Notchtop, but only the two easiest routes are included in this guide. The Southeast Gully and Northwest Ridge Route is the easiest descent route.

Notchtop is easily approached from Bear Lake. Follow the Fern Lake Trail past its junction with the Flattop Mountain Trail and continue west to 10,600 feet where the trail crosses the gentle saddle between Joe Mills Mountain and Flattop Mountain. This point is 2.8 miles from Bear Lake. Notchtop is easily seen from here. Lovely Lake Helene is 100 yards southwest of the trail, and there is a good spur trail leading to the lake.

Follow the spur trail around the north side of Lake Helene and pick up a faint, sometimes cairned trail leading up to the southwest from the west side of the lake. There are several versions of this unmaintained trail as it alternates

Notchtop Mountain from the southeast. July 4, 1987. The Southeast Gully is on the left, and the bottom part of the Spiral Route is visible below the sun-shadow ridge.

between rock slabs and patches of nasty bushes. The trail ends 0.4 miles southwest of Lake Helene by two small, unnamed lakes at 10,950 feet. Notchtop is now soaring overhead to the northwest.

Descent

Descend the Southeast Gully and Northwest Ridge Route.

Spiral Route II, Class 5.4 * Classic *

This classic route has been titillating climbers for years. It is well named as it spirals completely around the peak to reach the summit. This is a steep and committing route. Retreat can be difficult, and the exposure is often severe. Like all high-country rock climbs, this route rapidly becomes much more difficult when the weather turns against you. There is a lot of grass on the route, and after a summer hailstorm it becomes murderously slippery in slick-soled rock shoes.

From the unnamed lakes at 10,950 feet, head west up into the large southeast-facing gully under the south face of the peak. This gully is part of the Southeast Gully and Northwest Ridge Route and is not seen until the unnamed lakes are reached. From the point where cliffs are on both sides of you, ascend the gully for 200 feet. Leave the gully and angle up to the northeast (right) on a series of narrow ledges to a large bench above the initial cliffs of the southeast ridge. The route continues straight up the broken southeast ridge above this bench. This is a good place to rope up.

The challenge is met immediately. Climb up the steep

wall above the bench (5.4). Continue up an alternating series of broken areas and steep headwalls to a large, grassy ledge leading north across the steep east face. There is a total of four headwalls, and they are all 5.3–5.4. It is three pitches from the bench to the big, grassy ledge. The climbing on this part of the route is beautiful, and the rock has a solid, friendly countenance.

Traverse up to the north along the big, grassy ledge for 100 yards to an open area known as East Meadow on the northeast side of the peak. This traverse is Class 3 when it is dry, but the exposure here is extreme. A retreat back across this traverse can be very dangerous when it is wet.

East Meadow is below a 100-yard-wide, east-facing minicirque leading up to the namesake notch. The route continues up this minicirque for 500 feet to the notch. Above East Meadow, the climbing is broken Class 3 and Class 4 for 250 feet. The final 250 feet into the notch are steep and can look imposing at first. The difficult section can be overcome with one long or two shorter pitches. There are several spots of 5.4 and you need to read the rock carefully to stay on the easiest line; more difficult climbing lurks nearby. The rock here is smooth and shadowy, but there are some fixed pitons to cheer you up. The final scramble into the notch is Class 3.

From the notch, only the summit tower remains. Descend 30 feet south from the notch (Class 3), then scramble 80 feet up a northwest-facing, rubble-covered ramp (Class 3). From the top of the ramp, traverse north for 30 feet across some exposed Class 4 slabs, then continue north to the summit. Descend the Southeast Gully and Northwest Ridge Route.

Bad Variations
    There are three places in the minicirque where it is easy and tempting to head farther north. They are all wrong.
    1. The first temptation is when East Meadow is first entered as the big, grassy ledge continues north.
    2. The second temptation is 200 feet higher. The rock on the north (right) side of the minicirque becomes easy and allows rapid upward progress.
    3. The most-used temptation is 250 feet above East Meadow. There is an easy, east-facing gully on the north (right) side of the upper part of the minicirque. This gully is easy initially, but keeps pushing you north (right) as it becomes very steep higher up.
    If any of the temptations are taken, you will end up on an exposed platform 100 yards north of the notch. There is a nasty gap between this platform and the next tower west. For people over six feet tall, the dynamic step across this gap is 5.6. It is harder for shorter people. From the top of the tower west of the gap, downclimb 25 feet west into a notch (Class 4), climb 25 feet up the east-facing wall beyond (5.0–5.2) and traverse south to the notch (Class 4).

Southeast Gully and Northwest Ridge I, Class 4
    This is the easiest route to the summit of Notchtop. It is also the standard descent route. This route is circuitous and requires traversing above several hundred feet of the vertical south face of Notchtop. The traverse can be a nasty proposition when wet. Many parties carry a rope for this route. In any case bring your route-finding skills.

From the unnamed lakes at 10,950 feet, head west up into the large southeast-facing gully under the south face of the peak. This gully is not seen until the unnamed lakes are reached. Continue up the scree and grass in the gully and climb past an occasional Class 3 rock step. The very impressive south face of Notchtop rises right above this gully. Follow the gully all the way to its top at 12,100 feet in a notch on the northwest ridge of Notchtop. This is not the namesake notch of Notchtop. This notch is even with the summit and 200 yards northwest of it.

From the 12,100-foot notch, stay on the south side of the ridge and traverse southeast toward the summit on broken terrain. The initial part of the traverse stays well below the crest of the ridge. The exposure increases rapidly as you move out over the south face. There are two places where some Class 4 climbing is required, and the rest of the traverse is Class 3. The second, crux Class 4 traverse sneaks past the top of a gully and is maximally exposed. Once you are east of this gully, angle up east for 150 feet to the crest of the ridge. Scramble southeast on or near the ridge crest for another 150 feet (Class 3) and the summit will swing into view across the namesake notch. Descend a broken slope for 200 feet to the namesake notch.

From the namesake notch, only the summit tower remains. Descend 30 feet south from the notch (Class 3), then scramble 80 feet up a northwest-facing, rubble-covered ramp (Class 3). From the top of the ramp, traverse north for 30 feet across some exposed Class 4 slabs, then continue north to the summit.

Variation

The 12,100-foot notch on the northwest ridge at the top of the southeast gully can also be reached by descending from the Continental Divide. Descend from Point 12,280+ feet down a slope that is just north of the place where Notchtop's northwest ridge joins the divide. Point 12,280+ feet can be reached by hiking up the Flattop Mountain Trail from Bear Lake, continuing west from Flattop Mountain on the Tonahutu Creek Trail for 0.8 miles, then heading northeast along the divide for 0.6 miles. This approach is much longer but makes the climb slightly easier, as the ascent of the southeast gully is avoided.

Extra Credit

Climb the Southeast Gully and Northwest Ridge Route, then return to Bear Lake via the above variation. This makes a circle tour and allows you to bag Ptarmigan Point and Flattop Mountain in addition to Notchtop Mountain.

PTARMIGAN POINT 12,363 feet

This humble summit is on the Continental Divide 0.6 miles southwest of Notchtop Mountain and 0.8 miles west of Flattop Mountain. Ptarmigan Point should not be confused with Ptarmigan Mountain, which is several miles west of the divide above Lakes Nokoni and Nanita.

Ptarmigan Point rises no more than 202 vertical feet above Ptarmigan Pass, which is 300 yards south of the summit. The Tonahutu Creek Trail descends gently west from

Flattop Mountain, touches Ptarmigan Pass, then goes around Ptarmigan Point before descending into Tonahutu Creek. This summit excites little mountaineering interest when approached via this trail, as it is a simple, short hike above the trail. The mountaineering interest in this summit increases with an ascent of Ptarmigan Glacier southeast of the summit.

Ptarmigan Glacier I, Class 2, Easy/Moderate Snow
* Classic *

This permanent, northeast-facing snow slope provides an easy, fun route to the Continental Divide and Ptarmigan Point. It has the distinction of being one of only four easy routes to the Continental Divide in the entire Bear Lake area. Those four routes are Ptarmigan Glacier, Flattop Mountain Trail, Andrews Glacier and Stone Man Pass. Ptarmigan Glacier is slightly steeper than Andrews Glacier and gets icy in August. It should be approached with caution. An ice axe is recommended.

Follow the approach to the unnamed lakes at 10,950 feet described with Notchtop Mountain. Ptarmigan Glacier comes into view as the lakes are approached. There is a steep and ugly terminal moraine between these lakes and Ptarmigan Glacier. To avoid this moraine, hike south from the lakes toward Flattop Mountain and get onto the snow as soon as possible. In June there is snow all the way down to the unnamed lakes, and you can climb all the way to Ptarmigan Pass on snow.

As the steep North Side Couloirs of Flattop Mountain are approached, turn west (right) and ascend easy snow slopes under the couloirs and merge with Ptarmigan Glacier at 11,600 feet. The 200-yard wide glacier is an easy snow slope on its east edge and a moderate snow slope on its west edge. The steeper portions of this glacier are located above good runouts. Choose your line, have fun and climb up to Ptarmigan Pass at 12,180 feet. The summit of Ptarmigan Point is 300 yards north.

Descent

The descent is easily accomplished by hiking down the Flattop Mountain Trail. It is also easy to descend Ptarmigan Glacier. The walk down the east side of the glacier is easy and the glissade down the center of the glacier is great in June and July.

FLATTOP MOUNTAIN 12,324 feet

The expansive summit area of this peak is the largest in the park. Flattop is well named. This peak is on the Continental Divide 2.5 miles west of Bear Lake. Flattop has gentle east and west slopes, but its north and south faces are steep. This peak provides a surprising amount of good climbing.

Flattop Mountain Trail I, Class 1

Flattop is easily climbed by hiking up the Flattop Mountain Trail for 4.4 miles from Bear Lake. This scenic trail winds up the gentle eastern flank of the peak. Other than Milner Pass on Trail Ridge Road, this trail is the easiest

North Face Couloirs of Flattop Mountain. July 4, 1987.

way to reach the Continental Divide in Rocky Mountain National Park, and it is a very popular hike in the summer. The trail is often used as a descent route after ascents on neighboring peaks.

The highest point of Flattop Mountain is a six-foot boulder rising above the flatness. It is 200 feet south of the trail near the drop-off into Tyndall Gorge. Hard-core peak baggers may feel inclined to foot-coup this boulder, but they should do so with a smile and a chuckle for partners. Fangtop is yours!

North Face Couloirs I, Class 2, Steep Snow * Classic *

There are three permanent snow couloirs on the north face of Flattop which reach the summit plateau 0.4 miles west of the summit. A large snow slope connects the bottoms of these couloirs with Ptarmigan Glacier. Follow the approach to the unnamed lakes at 10,950 feet described with Notchtop Mountain. The couloirs and Ptarmigan Glacier come into view as the lakes are approached. The couloirs are south of the unnamed lakes and, in June, snow extends all the way down to the lakes. By September some ice forms in the couloirs. Climb south from the unnamed lakes to the broad snow slope at the base of the couloirs.

The eastern couloir provides the longest and easiest climb. Climb up the couloir for 600 feet on moderate snow, then engage the straightforward, steep finish that reaches an angle of 55 degrees. When snow conditions are good, this is a beautiful finish. The finish is 100 yards from the Flattop Mountain Trail, and your yodel might surprise a hiker!

The central and western couloirs are steeper than the

Otis Peak, Hallett Peak and Flattop Mountain from the east. October 21, 1987. From left to right: Otis Peak, Chaotic Glacier, Hallett Peak, Tyndall Glacier, Flattop Mountain.

eastern couloir, but they are much shorter. Both pass through narrow necks before opening out in their upper sections. These necks are the cruxes of the couloirs, and it is reasonable to place protection in the rock when passing through them.

Cornices are not usually a problem at the tops of these couloirs. Small cornices may form, but they can be avoided or climbed directly. Once you are on the summit plateau, it is a simple matter to descend via the Flattop Mountain Trail. This makes a nice Tour de Flattop. It is also easy to descend via Ptarmigan Glacier, permitting you to return to the base of your climb.

HALLETT PEAK 12,713 feet

Hallett Peak typifies the essence of Rocky Mountain National Park. It dominates the view to the west from Bear Lake, one of the most visited mountain lakes in Colorado. The steep north face of Hallett as seen in profile from Bear, Dream and Emerald lakes has stirred the hearts of many. The broken south face of Hallett rises above Chaos Canyon. The north face offers a plethora of serious technical routes. There is also a hiking route to the summit of Hallett. In between these two extremes are some moderate mountaineering routes providing a variety of challenges.

Northwest Slopes II, Class 2

This is the easiest route up Hallett. Start at Bear Lake and follow the Flattop Mountain Trail for 4.4 miles to the

Hallett Peak and the top of Tyndall Glacier. July 18, 1987.

summit of Flattop Mountain. From here, leave the trail and hike south, then southeast for 0.65 miles to the summit of Hallett. There are good views of the Tyndall Glacier on the traverse from Flattop to Hallett.

Tyndall Glacier II, Class 2, Moderate/Steep Snow
* Classic *

This is a fine mountaineering route in the heart of the park. Tyndall Glacier is at the west end of Tyndall Gorge. The approach up the gorge is very scenic, as it lies between the impressive north face of Hallett and the southern ramparts of Flattop. Tyndall Glacier is visible from Estes Park and appears on many postcards. Its easy visibility and access draw you into the picture. Don't forget your ice axe.

From Bear Lake, follow the Dream Lake Trail past Dream Lake and on to Emerald Lake. Continue on a rough trail around the south side of Emerald Lake. From the west end of Emerald Lake there are two choices for proceeding up into Tyndall Gorge. The easiest is to climb south to avoid some subsidiary cliffs and follow a talus alleyway up to the west. This alleyway is close under the north face of Hallett, and partway up it there is a narrow snow slope that can be used to avoid clambering over the large boulders in this area.

The second route into Tyndall Gorge heads straight up the steep slope west of Emerald Lake. The subsidiary cliffs must be dealt with on this route, and this is best done by finding a series of ledges allowing easy traverses to the south (left). The key traverse ledge through the main barrier cliff is high up, where the slope is turning into a gully on the steep south side of Flattop.

Once you are into the upper part of Tyndall Gorge, the large boulders under the north face of Hallett can be avoided by working up on a series of clean rock slabs on the Flattop (right) side of the gorge. Flowers abound in this area. At 11,600 feet, there is a small unnamed lake at the foot of the terminal moraine of Tyndall Glacier. This moraine is a mess, but can be easily avoided by following a small gully up to the southwest. This gully retains snow well into the summer and provides an easy route to the base of Tyndall Glacier.

Tyndall Glacier is several hundred yards wide and offers a variety of ascent routes. The northern and central portions reach 35 degrees and are 400 feet high. The southern portion is 500 feet high, steepens to 45 degrees and contains some interesting crevasses near the top. These crevasses are surprisingly large for Colorado. On the extreme southeast edge of the glacier is a separate gully that offers the longest and steepest line of ascent. You can also avoid the glacier entirely by scrambling up some rubble-covered ledges on the north side of the glacier. Choose your line and have fun.

Once you are on the Continental Divide, hike 0.4 miles southeast to the summit of Hallett Peak. Descend the Northwest Slopes Route. In midsummer your ascent of Tyndall Glacier is likely to attract the attention of hikers on the Flattop Mountain Trail. If you want an audience, this is a good route!

East Ridge II, Class 5.3–5.4

This route is an interesting and scenic hike interrupted by two pitches of technical climbing. Start at Bear Lake and follow the Lake Haiyaha Trail toward Lake Haiyaha. Leave the trail at 10,200 feet as it climbs south around the lower east ridge of Hallett and climb west to the crest of the ridge. Continue west along the craggy ridge for 0.75 miles to 11,100 feet where the ridge bumps into a cliff band.

This cliff band is connected to the first buttress on the north face and also extends for several hundred yards on the south side of the peak. It cannot be avoided and must be climbed. The cliff band is not as steep as it first appears, and there are a number of places where it can be climbed. The easiest places are close to the ridge crest on the south side of the ridge. The cliff band can be overcome with two moderate-length pitches of 5.3–5.4 climbing.

Once you are above the cliff band, hike west for 0.8 miles to the summit. This hike takes you along the top of the great north face of Hallett, and a lot of Big Air lives around here. Descending the Northwest Slopes Route completes a nice Tour de Hallett.

OTIS PEAK 12,486 feet

This peak forms part of the magnificent mountain sky-line above Estes Park. It is on the Continental Divide 0.8 miles south of Hallett Peak and 0.5 miles northeast of Andrews Pass. Otis Peak has gentle east and west slopes and very steep north and south faces. The peak rises in the midst of mountain splendor, as it is bounded by Chaos Canyon to the north and Loch Vale to the south. The summit is easily reached once you are on the Continental Divide. The trick is getting up there, and the glaciers at the head of Chaos

Canyon and Loch Vale provide a great means of ascent.

Chaotic Glacier II, Class 2, Moderate Snow * Classic *

This permanent snowfield resides at the west end of Chaos Canyon. Chaotic Glacier is visible from Estes Park, and it is easy to preview snow conditions before your climb. This glacier is best done in June and July, as a gap forms in it during August. Conditions were still ideal on my July 18 ascent. From Bear Lake, hike west on the Dream Lake Trail. Two hundred yards east of Dream Lake, turn south (left) and follow the trail to Lake Haiyaha. This lake is at the east end of Chaos Canyon, and Chaotic Glacier is visible from here.

There is no trail into Chaos Canyon, and this valley has a bad reputation for being an impenetrable mess of house-sized boulders. There is indeed a house-sized boulder on the south shore of Lake Haiyaha, and you can get tuned up by ascending its south face! In fact, the 1.5-mile hike up Chaos Canyon is rough, but it is not all that bad. You will be rewarded with solitude.

As you head west from Lake Haiyaha, the challenge is met immediately. There are a lot of, ahem, car-sized boulders in this area. Persevere and move to the south (left) side of the canyon, close under the slopes of Otis. There are some easier slopes here. Halfway up the canyon, there is a significant snow slope on the south side of the canyon that allows passage past the largest area of house-sized boulders. Just west of this snow slope at 11,000 feet is a small, beautiful unnamed lake. Chaotic Glacier is now visible, including its large lower arm extending north toward Hallett

Chaotic Glacier. July 18, 1987.

Peak. The bottom of the glacier is 0.3 miles west of the un-named lake. The northern ramparts of Otis are impressive from here.

The ascent up the glacier is fun and a fitting reward after the approach up Chaos Canyon. The slope is easy at first and gradually steepens to 35 degrees. The steep portion is not very long, as the glacier rounds gently up to the Continental Divide. There are no cornices at the top, only alpine flowers. The summit of Otis is an easy 0.4-mile hike southeast. The quickest descent is via Andrews Glacier, but you can also hike north over Hallett Peak and descend the Flattop Mountain Trail.

Andrews Glacier II, Class 2, Easy Snow * Classic *

This is one of the easier routes to the Continental Divide in Rocky Mountain National Park and is often used as a descent route. It is a very scenic hike through Loch Vale and the heartland of the park. Andrews Glacier is gentle and recommended for first-time visitors who would like to understand the lay of the land better.

From the Glacier Gorge Trailhead, follow the Loch Vale Trail to the Loch at 10,200 feet. This is one of the nicest places in the park. After going around the north side of the Loch, continue west for 0.4 miles to a stream crossing. This is Andrews Creek. The trail to Andrews Glacier leaves the Loch Vale Trail and heads north along the west side of Andrews Creek. The creek and trail soon turn west and climb through an enchanted forest to treeline at the foot of the Gash. The Gash is a north-facing side valley leading up to the impressive Sharkstooth.

The trail to Andrews Glacier does not go into the Gash, but crosses to the north side of Andrews Creek and climbs west across a rough talus field. The trail returns to the south side of the creek and climbs steeply up to Andrews Tarn at 11,600 feet. This lake is right at the bottom of Andrews Glacier. In fact, the glacier ends in the lake. Sliding down the glacier into Andrews Tarn would tarnish your climb!

It is easy to avoid this water hazard. Hike around the south side of Andrews Tarn and continue up on the easy south side of the glacier. Andrews Glacier averages 20 degrees and is a hike that just happens to take place on snow. It is steeper in the center section, then rounds up gracefully to Andrews Pass on the Continental Divide at 12,000 feet. The summit of Otis Peak is an easy 0.5-mile hike northeast up grass and talus.

Extra Credit

The summit of Taylor Peak (13,153 feet) is an easy 1-mile hike south from Andrews Pass.

7 GLACIER GORGE

This chapter covers the peaks on or east of the Continental Divide between Andrews Pass and Pagoda Mountain. This stretch of the divide embraces the Loch Vale and Glacier Gorge cirques. These valleys are not just in the heart of the park, they are in the hearts of all who visit them. The scenery here is magnificent. The approach to this area is on maintained trails that start at the Glacier Gorge Trailhead. The following U.S.G.S. quadrangles cover this area: Mc-Henrys Peak, Longs Peak, Isolation Peak and Allens Park.

Five important thirteeners are covered in this chapter, and they are some of the harder peaks to climb in this book. Some consider McHenrys to be the hardest peak in Rocky Mountain National Park. Many mountaineers have tested their skills on these faces. Rock, snow and ice: it's all here.

SHARKSTOOTH 12,630+ feet

This magnificent peak is well named. After climbing in Colorado for over 30 years I am still startled every time I spot Sharkstooth, as it often blends in with the east face of Taylor Peak. There are times when clouds obscure Taylor and Sharkstooth is seen acutely. I always think to myself, Wow! Look at THAT!

North face of Sharkstooth. July 5, 1987. The East Col is on the left. The Northeast Ridge is not the left skyline. It is right of the East Col and leads to the large bench on the left skyline.

Sharkstooth is a freestanding pinnacle 0.3 miles east of the Continental Divide on a complicated ridge running northeast from Taylor Peak. This ridge separates the Andrews Glacier drainage from upper Loch Vale. Sharkstooth is easily approached and the technical routes on it are excellent. There is no walk-up route to the summit of Sharkstooth. This peak is reserved for climbers.

To approach Sharkstooth, follow the Andrews Glacier Route described with Otis Peak. Leave this route at treeline (10,700 feet) and climb south up into the Gash. The Gash is a well-named, steep defile 0.6 miles long. Sharkstooth looms profoundly at its south end. Near the bottom of the Gash, move to its west (right) side to avoid some cliffs. There is a moderate snow slope here through June. Higher up, ascend talus on the east (left) side of the Gash to reach the northeast side of Sharkstooth.

Descent

This is not a good peak to be on top of without a rope. Rappel and downclimb the East Gully Route. There is a fixed rappel anchor at the top of the summit cliff. Do one rappel down the summit cliff, then scramble down to the lowest point on the north side of the meadow. Two more rappels plus some scrambling take you down to the east col. Scramble north down the couloir below the east col and descend the Gash to the trail.

Northeast Ridge II, Class 5.6 * Classic *

This is one of a handful of routes that reigns larger than life. The route ascends a small, broken ridge on the northeast side of Sharkstooth. Steep, exposed climbing and a magnificent setting combine to produce an unprecedented experience. From the upper reaches of the Gash, head south up into the north-facing couloir leading to the col on the east side of Sharkstooth. Do not ascend all the way to the east col. The route starts 300 feet below the col.

The northeast ridge does not extend all the way down to the couloir. Climb a long 5.6 pitch up to a wide, grassy ledge and traverse north (right) on this ledge to the base of the ridge. Ascend the ridge for four or five pitches to a distinct shoulder that is high on the ridge. The climbing on the ridge is broken and any serious obstacles can be avoided by moving to the southeast (left) side of the ridge. With careful route-finding, the difficulty on the ridge does not exceed 5.4 and the cruxes are short. From the shoulder, two more 5.0–5.2 pitches ascend the final, spectacular ridge to the summit.

East Gully II, Class 5.4 * Classic *

This is the easiest route to the summit of Sharkstooth and is the standard descent route. The climbing is steep and enjoyable, especially near the summit. This route is recommended for people looking for a technical route to a decisive summit.

From the upper reaches of the Gash, ascend the north-facing couloir that leads to the col on the east side of Sharkstooth (Class 3). There is moderate snow in this couloir through July and an ice axe is recommended. You can avoid the snow by climbing the rocks on the west (right) side of the couloir (Class 4).

From the east col, a broad gully leads west up the peak. This is the route. Scramble up the gully and climb to the base of a headwall (5.0–5.2). Climb up the middle of the 5.4 headwall and continue up a series of short 5.0–5.2 steps between ledges to a lower, angled meadow. Scramble up 200 feet to the top of the meadow and the base of the final summit cliff (Class 3). Climb 60 feet up the final cliff near its south (left) edge via some cracks just north of a spectacular and exposed ridge (5.4). Voila! Le summit.

Variation

The final summit cliff can be climbed by a less-exposed 5.4 route near the center of the small east face. This route starts up 5.0–5.2 rock in the center of the face, then steps south (left) to reach the final 30 feet and the 5.4 crux.

TAYLOR PEAK 13,153 feet

Taylor Peak is on the Continental Divide 3.2 miles southwest of Bear Lake. Taylor has the distinction of being Colorado's northernmost thirteener on the Continental Divide. It is a large peak with gentle north, west and south slopes. It has a very steep east face which stands in sharp contrast to the rest of the peak. Taylor is a good example of differential glaciation.

North Slopes II, Class 2, Easy Snow

Taylor is easily climbed by following the Andrews Glacier Route described with Otis Peak. From Andrews

Pass, climb south for a gentle mile up grass and talus to the summit. This is also the best descent route.

Taylor Glacier II, Class 3, Steep Snow/Ice * Classic *

This is a very good snow climb, which offers up to 1,200 vertical feet of snow climbing. Taylor Glacier is a permanent snow slope, which reaches the Continental Divide 0.5 miles south of the summit. The upper part of the glacier is visible from many points to the east, so it is easy to preview conditions on this route.

From the Glacier Gorge Trailhead, follow the Loch Vale Trail to the Loch at 10,200 feet. Go around the north side of the loch and continue on the rough, unmaintained trail past Glass Lake to Sky Pond at 10,900 feet. Taylor Glacier is visible to the southwest from here. Go around the north side of Sky Pond and climb up to the base of the glacier at 11,400 feet.

Taylor Glacier is quite broad at the bottom but it narrows to a 30-foot-wide couloir at the top. It is very gentle at the bottom but steepens to 60 degrees at the top. This is a glacier of contrasts. Carefully study the condition of the summit cornice before heading up the glacier. It can completely block the direct finish. It is because of this route that Taylor has been called the "moderate my ass glacier"!

Climb up the glacier as it relentlessly steepens. The dump gullies on this glacier can become five feet deep, and crossing them can be difficult. A three-foot wide-snow/rock chimney sometimes forms on the north side of the summit cornice and allows a direct finish. The snow below

Taylor Glacier from Sky Pond. July 5, 1987.

the cornice is 60 degrees in any case. Once you are on the divide, the summit is an easy 0.5-mile hike up to the north. Descend via Andrews Glacier.

Variations
1. Two hundred fifty feet below the cornice, a branch couloir heads up to the north (right). This couloir is slightly less steep than the direct finish and does not have such a large cornice at its top. It makes a good alternate finish if you do not like what you see straight up.
2. The most spectacular finish of all is 100 feet south of the direct finish. It ascends a slender, 70-degree rib of snow.

THATCHTOP 12,668 feet

Thatchtop is the large peak east of the Continental Divide between Loch Vale and Glacier Gorge. It is 2.3 miles south of Bear Lake and dominates much of the view in this direction. The upper north slope of Thatchtop is a huge talus field while the lower slopes of the peak are steep and rugged. Thatchtop excites little mountaineering interest but does provide access to the northeast ridge of Powell Peak.

Northeast Slopes II, Class 2
This is the easiest route to the summit of Thatchtop. From the Glacier Gorge Trailhead, follow the Loch Vale Trail to its junction with the Glacier Gorge Trail. Follow the Glacier Gorge Trail for 200 yards to the bridge across Icy Brook. Leave the trail and hike west along Icy Brook for 100

yards, then bushwhack up the hillside to the south. Ascend a gully system through the lower cliffs to the easy upper slopes. Climb south up talus for 0.8 miles to the summit.

POWELL PEAK 13,208 feet

This shy peak is on the Continental Divide 1 mile southeast of Taylor Peak and 0.5 miles northwest of McHenrys Peak. Powell is not easily seen as a distinct summit. From most vantage points, it is largely hidden by the bland mass of Thatchtop. Powell has a gentle southwest slope, a steep north face and a ferocious east face. This peak provides some interesting routes.

West Slopes II, Class 2, Easy Snow

This is the easiest route on Powell. Follow the Andrews Glacier Route on Otis Peak to Andrews Pass. From here, hike south and either climb Taylor Peak or skirt it to the west. From Taylor, continue southeast for a long mile to the summit of Powell. This is a long hike, but there are no technical difficulties. This is also the best descent route.

North Face II, Class 2, Moderate/Steep Snow/Ice
* Classic *

The north face of Powell Peak rises above Sky Pond and contains a series of long snow couloirs. Follow the approach to Sky Pond described with the Taylor Glacier Route on Taylor Peak. The couloirs are visible to the south from here. The easternmost couloir provides a long, moder-

North Face of Powell Peak. July 5, 1987.

ate climb while the western couloirs provide steep challenges. The snow in these couloirs lasts through July and turns to ice late in the summer. Crampons are recommended after July 1.

Hike up above the south side of Sky Pond to the bottom of the snow and choose your climb. The easternmost couloir reaches the divide without cornices at 13,000 feet. The summit is 250 yards south.

Northeast Ridge II, Class 4

This is the long, jagged ridge connecting Powell to Thatchtop. Follow Thatchtop's Northeast Slopes Route to the summit of Thatchtop. From here, follow the ridge for a mile to the Continental Divide. The summit of Powell is 200 yards south. The ridge is easy initially but soon becomes very exposed. It is steep on the northwest side and nearly vertical on the southeast side. There are some stretches of Class 4 climbing and a rope is recommended for this route.

ARROWHEAD 12,640+ feet

This peak is the high point of a ridge running northeast for 0.5 miles from McHenrys Peak. Arrowhead is 0.5 miles west of Black Lake and forms the west end of the great wall that rings upper Glacier Gorge. The peak has sections of beautiful rock, but is mostly broken and ledge ridden.

Northwest Face II, Class 3

This is the easiest route on Arrowhead and provides an interesting mountaineering ascent. From the Glacier Gorge Trailhead, follow the Loch Vale Trail to its junction with the Glacier Gorge Trail. Follow the Glacier Gorge Trail south for 2 miles to a meadow at 10,240 feet. Leave the trail and bushwhack west up a steep slope to Solitude Lake at 11,400 feet. The steep north face of Arrowhead rises directly above the south side of the lake. Solitude Lake is well named and you are not likely to see anyone else here.

Continue west up the gentle valley above Solitude Lake for 0.3 miles to 11,550 feet. From here, there are good views of the seldom-seen east face of Powell Peak and north face of McHenrys Peak. The easiest route up Arrowhead is not immediately obvious as continuous cliff bands link the north faces of Arrowhead and McHenrys. Directly below the Arrowhead-McHenrys saddle is a gully that starts easily, but ends in a deep hole. This is not the route. One hundred yards northeast (left) of this gully is a smaller gully/crack system. Ascend this weakness for 150 feet and then do an ascending traverse southwest (right) on a series of large ledges. Climb straight up another crack system to a talus slope above the face.

McHENRYS PEAK 13,327 feet

This wonderful peak is on the Continental Divide and forms the western ramparts of upper Glacier Gorge. McHenrys Peak is the most difficult peak over 13,000 feet in Rocky Mountain National Park and is a test piece for peak baggers. McHenrys Peak has a beautiful east face and is aesthetically pleasing to look at. It has steep but broken north and west faces. Between the north and west faces is McHenrys Notch on the Continental Divide. McHenrys Notch is one of the serious obstacles to walking right along the crest of the divide. Only on its south side does McHenrys relent, but these slopes can still provide plenty of excitement.

McHenrys is approached from the Glacier Gorge Trailhead. Follow the Loch Vale Trail to its junction with the Glacier Gorge Trail and then follow the Glacier Gorge Trail south up into Glacier Gorge. Any route on McHenrys provides a long day, and many tired feet have plodded back to the Glacier Gorge Trailhead with greater respect for this peak.

Arrowhead Arete II, Class 4

This route ascends the ridge connecting McHenrys with Arrowhead. It is a long climb and is harder than the Stone Man Pass Route. The route is steep and exposed in places and a rope is recommended.

From the Loch Vale–Glacier Gorge trail junction, follow the Glacier Gorge Trail south for 2 miles to a meadow at 10,240 feet. Leave the trail and bushwhack west

East face of McHenrys Peak. September 13, 1987. The Stone Man is on the far left. Stone Man Pass is left of the summit and the Arrowhead Arete is right of the

up a steep slope to Solitude Lake at 11,400 feet. Solitude Lake is well named and you are not likely to see anyone else here. Continue west up the gentle valley above Solitude Lake for 0.3 miles to 11,550 feet. From here, there are good views of the seldom-seen east face of Powell Peak and north face of McHenrys Peak.

Follow Arrowhead's Northwest Face Route through Class 3 cliff bands, then ascend directly to the Arrowhead-McHenrys saddle. From the saddle, climb southwest up the ridge toward two large towers. Stay well below the ridge and bypass both towers on the northwest (right) side of the ridge (some Class 4). Beyond the towers, the ridge steepens. Ascend Class 4 slabs up a shallow gully 150 feet northwest of the ridge crest to reach the summit.

Stone Man Pass II, Class 3 * Classic *

This is the easiest route to the summit of McHenrys. When the route is dry it is an easy scramble, but when it is wet or snow covered it becomes much more serious. In any case this is a long climb. From the Loch Vale–Glacier Gorge trail junction, follow the rough Glacier Gorge Trail south for 2.6 miles to Black Lake at 10,600 feet. Black Lake is nearly ringed with cliffs, and here the adventure begins.

The easiest way to get above the cliffs ringing Black Lake is to follow a trail east for 0.3 miles up a small valley directly east of the lake. At 11,000 feet, head south and get up onto the broad bench above the cliffs. This route is easy, but it takes you away from McHenrys.

You can also climb west above Black Lake and breach the cliffs. Study this route carefully before attempting it.

Ascend a crack up a slab, then traverse south (left) across some higher slabs to easier ground. When wet, these slabs can be very difficult, and the longer eastern route is the safer choice.

From the bench above Black Lake, head west toward the slopes leading to Stone Man Pass. The bench above Black Lake alternates between rock slabs and nasty bushes and requires some mini-route-finding. Stone Man is a rock tower on the ridge between McHenrys Peak and Chiefs Head Peak. Stone Man is easily visible from the bench above Black Lake. Stone Man Pass is north of Stone Man just below the steeper, southeast ridge of McHenrys. Stone Man Pass is not the low point of the ridge between McHenrys and Chiefs Head.

Climb a steep, rubble-filled, northeast-facing gully to Stone Man Pass. Some Class 3 scrambling may be required to reach the pass. In June and early July, snow in this gully aids or hinders your effort depending on the condition of the snow. Early June snow in this gully has a reputation for avalanching, and this route is not recommended before June 15.

From Stone Man Pass, do a long ascending traverse northwest to reach a gap in a southwest-facing rib (some Class 3). Finding this gap is the key to this route. Cross the rib and get into the small basin west of the rib. This basin is snow filled and dangerous in early June. Climb north up the small basin to the crest of McHenrys' southeast ridge at 13,200 feet. Follow the ridge northwest for 100 yards to the summit.

Variation

Stone Man Pass is easily reached from Lake Powell on the west side of the divide, but a long trailless hike is required to reach Lake Powell. McHenrys is rarely approached from the west.

SPEARHEAD 12,575 feet

This peak is nestled in the shadow of Chiefs Head Peak in the heart of Glacier Gorge. The unbroken sweeps of rock on this peak set it apart from its statuesque neighbors. The triangular northeast face of Spearhead is one of the most beautiful rock walls in Colorado. Spearhead also has a remarkable summit. Spearhead is 1 mile west of Longs Peak and 0.5 miles north of Chiefs Head Peak. Because of its proximity to these giants, Spearhead is often overlooked, but this should not be the case. The finest rock climb in this guide is on Spearhead.

The approach to Spearhead starts at the Glacier Gorge Trailhead. Follow the Loch Vale Trail to its junction with the Black Lake Trail. Follow the rough Black Lake Trail south past Mills Lake to Black Lake at 10,600 feet. Black Lake is nearly ringed with cliffs and is a special place. From the east side of Black Lake, climb east up a small valley on a trail. At 11,000 feet, head south and get onto the large bench north of Spearhead. This bench alternates between clean rock slabs and nasty bushes. The easiest way across is not obvious on a first encounter, but a little route-finding takes you south to the base of the north ridge of Spearhead

Northeast face of Spearhead. September 13, 1987. The North Ridge is on the right of the face.

at 11,600 feet. This is a long approach.

North Ridge III, Class 5.6 * Classic *

This climb reminds me of why I started climbing in the first place. It is fundamental. It is magnificent. The climb takes place on rock so solid that you feel like you are touching the soul of the earth. Touch it. Climb it!

The north ridge of Spearhead separates the unbroken sweep of the northeast face from the more broken northwest face. The north ridge is not well defined and is really a narrow face. The route ascends directly up the center of this small face, then angles east (left) near the top of the wall for a spectacular finish. The protection possibilities on this route are excellent.

The climb starts on a grassy ledge at the base of the face. If the climb is done roped from this point, it requires eight or nine pitches. This is a long and committing climb. The lower part of the face is steep and has an obvious chimney in it. This chimney is broken, and there are actually two chimneys side by side. They are not proper chimneys but, rather, broken crack systems at the back of an indentation.

Climb a 120-foot pitch up the initial slabs to a secure stance 40 feet below the eastern chimney (5.0–5.2). The second 150-foot pitch climbs directly up the eastern chimney and continues up the crack above it (5.4). The chimney is steep but broken and there are lots of holds. The third pitch continues straight up the crack system for another 150 feet (5.3). There are two curious, V-shaped slots on this pitch separated by 40 feet of easy climbing.

From the top of the third pitch, the upper wall is visible. The center third of the climb consists of low-angle slabs. There are several ways to proceed upward. The easiest route angles slightly west (right) and ascends a small Class 3 gully for 100 feet before angling back east (left) into the center of the face. Time can be saved by scrambling up this section unroped.

The upper part of the wall sweeps up to near-vertical and contains the most enjoyable climbing of the route. From the top of the scrambling section, ascend a 150-foot pitch up and slightly east (left) across beautiful, clean slabs (5.0–5.2). Aim for a long crack system in the center of the face that ascends toward the near-vertical, upper wall. Climb another 150-foot pitch up this steepening crack to a stance below a large block (5.0–5.2).

The top part of the narrow north face is higher on its eastern end and consists of several east-angling cracks and grooves. The steep slabs between these cracks form barriers to a direct finish. From the stance below the block, climb straight up to the block (5.5), go around the west (right) side of the block and ascend an eight-foot-wide, east-angling groove behind the block. Find a secure stance above the block. This pitch is 110 feet long.

The final pitch is the hardest and most spectacular on the climb. Continue angling east (left) on a narrowing ramp until it sweeps up into a small dihedral. This dihedral is very near the ridge between the northeast face and the now very narrow north face. Climb up the dihedral for 30 feet to a very exposed position (5.4). The sweeps of both the north and northeast faces are now below your heels. The crux is above you, but it is short. Climb 10 feet up a steep, awkward slot right on the crest of the ridge to the top of the wall (5.6). This final pitch is 120 feet long.

The summit is 300 feet of Class 3 scrambling above the top of the wall. Stay on the west side of the ridge for this final scramble. Descend via the Northwest Slopes Route.

Variation

After the third pitch, move east (left) or continue straight up and rejoin the regular route for its last pitch.

Northwest Slopes II, Class 3

This is the easiest route to the spectacular summit of Spearhead. From the base of the north ridge, hike southwest toward Frozen Lake. Do not go all the way to Frozen Lake, but get on a bench between the northwest face of Spearhead and the lake. Hike south on this bench below all the cliffs of the northwest face. Ascend a long and very loose scree gully to the Spearhead–Chiefs Head saddle at 12,300 feet. Stay on the west side of Spearhead's south ridge and traverse north to the summit (Class 3). A little route-finding is required to avoid the small cliffs in this area. Stay well below the ridge crest. The final moves out to the highest point are only Class 3, but they are very exposed. Whee!

Variation

You can avoid the loose scree gully by scrambling directly up the northwest slopes to the summit (Class 3). This is a shorter, more difficult route.

CHIEFS HEAD PEAK 13,579 feet

Chiefs Head is the third highest peak in Rocky Mountain National Park and it carries this distinction well. Its summit is 200 yards east of the Continental Divide above vast northeast and north faces that guard the south end of Glacier Gorge. When Chiefs Head is viewed from the northwest, these great faces are seen in profile and the peak looks out of place for the Rocky Mountains. It looks positively exotic and appears imported from Baffin Island.

The approach used for Chiefs Head depends on the route. The peak can be approached either from Glacier Gorge or Wild Basin. A one-day ascent of Chiefs Head is a long day. It is easier to climb this peak with a high camp.

Northwest Ridge II, Class 3

This is the easiest route up Chiefs Head from Glacier Gorge. This route is long but presents no great technical difficulties. Follow the Stone Man Pass Route on McHenrys Peak to Stone Man Pass. Descend slightly on the west side of Stone Man Pass, then traverse south on the west side of the ridge to avoid the gendarmes right on the ridge. An ugly section of broken cliffs appears to block access to the easy talus slope on the west side of Chiefs Head, and these cliffs are the crux of the route. With a little route-finding in gullies, you can climb through these cliffs with Class 3 scrambling. The summit is 0.6 miles southeast up a narrowing talus slope.

Northeast Face Ramp II, Class 4, Moderate Snow

This is a peculiar route up a huge ramp on a huge face. The Northeast Face of Chiefs Head is the face east of the Spearhead–Chiefs Head ridge, and it has an obvious ramp angling across it which holds snow through the summer. This is the route. The trick is getting to it.

Follow the Northwest Slopes Route on Spearhead to the Spearhead–Chiefs Head col. The upper part of the ramp is visible from here. Cross to the east side of the col, descend slightly and ascend south up the obvious ramp. One hundred yards up the ramp is a small shoulder, and the crux of the route is visible from here. There is a section where the ramp has disintegrated into a series of small ledges. Some Class 4 climbing on very loose rock is required to traverse across this section to the broad upper part of the ramp.

Once you are on the upper ramp, it is hard to get lost. Ascend the wide, moderate snow slope on the ramp to the east ridge of Chiefs Head at 13,350 feet. The ramp gets steeper toward the top but does not exceed 45 degrees. The ramp goes above a large portion of the north face and there is still a lot of virtual exposure on the wide ramp. Once you are on the east ridge, scramble up big talus blocks for 300 yards to the summit. Descending the Northwest Ridge Route makes a nice Tour de Chiefs Head.

Chiefs Head–Pagoda Couloir II, Class 2, Steep Snow
* Classic *

This route ascends the obvious, north-facing couloir below the Chiefs Head–Pagoda col. This straightforward couloir holds some snow through the summer, but is in the best condition in July. The couloir rises between the two large, solid north faces of Chiefs Head and Pagoda. The feeling in here is very alpine.

Refer to Spearhead for directions to the bench above Black Lake at 11,100 feet. The route is visible from this bench. Hike south around the east side of Spearhead to the base of the couloir and ascend it for 850 vertical feet to the col. From the col, scramble west up large talus blocks for 0.6 miles to the summit. Stay slightly on the south side of the east ridge. Descending via the Northwest Ridge Route makes a nice Tour de Chiefs Head and eliminates the need to descend this steep couloir.

Southeast Slopes II, Class 2

This is a straightforward hiking route on the south side of Chiefs Head. It is a 16-mile round-trip with 5,100 vertical feet of elevation gain. From the Wild Basin Trailhead, follow the Thunder Lake Trail to its junction with the Lion Lake Trail. Follow the Lion Lake Trail northwest for another 1.5 miles to the first Lion Lake at 11,060 feet. Leave the trail, head east and ascend a scree gully for 400 vertical feet to the open talus slopes southeast of Chiefs Head at 11,800 feet. From here, the summit of Chiefs Head is 1.3 miles up to the northwest. It's a long way up this final slope, but there are no difficulties.

West Slopes II, Class 2

This is the easiest route to the summit of Chiefs Head, but it is an 18-mile round-trip with 5,100 vertical feet of elevation gain. From the Wild Basin Trailhead, follow the

Thunder Lake Trail to its junction with the Lion Lake Trail. Follow the Lion Lake Trail northwest for another 1.5 miles to the first Lion Lake at 11,060 feet. Continue northwest past the second Lion Lake to Snowbank Lake at 11,521 feet. The rugged southwest face of Chiefs Head is above this lake, and it prevents direct access to the summit.

Continue northwest for another mile, hiking up a faint, unmaintained trail to the broad saddle between Chiefs Head and Mount Alice at 12,450 feet. From here, the summit is another mile back to the east up the talus-covered west slopes of Chiefs Head. This face narrows to a ridge at the top and what little excitement this route offers is reserved for this final ridge.

PAGODA MOUNTAIN 13,497 feet

This triangular peak has three ridges, three faces and a good name. It is 0.7 miles southwest of Longs Peak and 0.8 miles east of Chiefs Head Peak. Together with its higher and larger neighbor, Chiefs Head, it guards the south end of Glacier Gorge. The north and southwest faces of Pagoda are steep and serious. The west ridge between these two faces is difficult and makes it impractical to climb both Pagoda and Chiefs Head together. Easy access to the summit is found on Pagoda's east face. Like Chiefs Head, Pagoda can be climbed from either the north or the south. Both these routes finish on the northeast ridge.

Pagoda is connected to Longs Peak by a beautiful,

tower-ridden ridge known as the Keyboard of the Winds. You can climb Pagoda together with Longs. See the Grand Slam for information on how to do this.

Northwest Face and Northeast Ridge II, Class 3

This is the easiest route up Pagoda from Glacier Gorge. It climbs from Glacier Gorge to the Longs-Pagoda col. Refer to Spearhead for directions to the bench above Black Lake at 11,100 feet. The route is visible from this bench. Hike southeast past the east side of Spearhead to Green Lake. From Green Lake, climb southeast up 1,500 vertical feet of scree and slabs to the Longs-Pagoda col at 13,100 feet. This ascent is slabby and a bit steep near the top, but the difficulty does not exceed Class 3. From the col, climb southwest up talus for 300 yards on the southeast side of Pagoda's northeast ridge to the summit.

Southeast Basin and Northeast Ridge II, Class 2

This is the easiest route to the summit of Pagoda. It approaches the peak from the Copeland Lake Trailhead and requires 5,150 vertical feet of elevation gain. Follow the Keplinger's Couloir Route on Longs Peak to 12,000 feet in the high basin formed by Mount Meeker, Longs and Pagoda. Hike northwest up the basin, skirt some cliffs on their east side, and climb west to the Longs-Pagoda col at 13,100 feet. From the col, climb southwest up talus for 300 yards on the southeast side of Pagoda's northeast ridge to the summit.

8 LONGS PEAK

This chapter covers just four peaks, and there is very little to say about two of them. The other two, Longs Peak and Mount Meeker, combine to produce the most magnificent mountain cirque in Colorado.

Longs and Meeker are the two highest peaks in Rocky Mountain National Park, and Longs is probably climbed more often than all the other peaks in this book combined! Many of this book's best climbs are on Longs and Meeker, and this is one of the larger chapters in the book. If you don't know what all the hullabaloo is about, then perhaps it's time for you to visit Longs and Meeker! The following U.S.G.S. quadrangles cover this area: Longs Peak and Allenspark.

STORM PEAK 13,326 feet

This humble summit has lived in the shadow of mighty Longs Peak for a long time. Storm Peak is 0.8 miles northwest of Longs and 0.3 miles west of the Boulder Field. Thousands of people have tramped by on their way to Longs, but very few take the time to climb Storm. This peak must be lonely and would probably appreciate your visit. Refer to the Keyhole Route on Longs Peak for directions to the Boulder Field and the Keyhole.

East Slopes II, Class 2

The easiest way to climb Storm is to hike west from the Boulder Field and ascend steep, sometimes loose talus to the summit.

Variation

You can also traverse north on the east side of the Keyhole Ridge for 0.4 miles from the Keyhole and reach the summit of Storm. This route allows Storm to be climbed after an ascent of Longs. It is best to give up some elevation when traversing north from the Keyhole to avoid some nasty sections of talus. Remember that the summit of Storm is the point farthest north. Don't cut up too soon.

MOUNT LADY WASHINGTON 13,281 feet

This peak is 0.7 miles northeast of Longs and 0.4 miles east of the Boulder Field. For the most part, it is a featureless mass of talus, but the view of the east face of Longs from the summit makes an ascent of Lady Washington worthwhile. Refer to Longs Peak for directions to the Boulder Field.

East Slopes II, Class 2

From the Longs Peak Trailhead, hike up the East Longs Peak Trail for 3.8 miles to the trail junction at 11,550 feet on the Mills Moraine. The shortest route to the summit of Lady Washington leaves the trail here and climbs straight west for 0.8 miles up talus to the summit. This is a long talus slope and many souls have cursed it.

Northwest Slopes II, Class 2

Lady Washington is easily climbed from the Boulder Field. From the Boulder Field at 12,750 feet, climb southeast up talus for 0.4 miles to the summit. This is a much shorter distance across talus than the East Slopes Route. This route is the logical way to climb Lady Washington after an ascent of Longs.

Camel II, Class 2

There is a south-facing, Class 2 gully west of the summit of Lady Washington connecting the Chasm Lake area with the Boulder Field area. This gully is called the Camel, and it ascends from 12,400 feet elevation west of Chasm Lake to the Lady Washington–Longs saddle at 13,000 feet. The Camel Route is most often used by climbers descending Longs who wish to return to Chasm Lake.

LONGS PEAK 14,255 feet

Longs Peak is unquestionably the monarch of the park. It dominates all that is within sight of it. Longs Peak is the highest peak in Rocky Mountain National Park and Boulder County. It is also the northernmost fourteener in Colorado and the Rocky Mountains. Its summit attracts thousands of people each year, and it is one of the more popular peaks in the western United States. The reason for the popularity is obvious. Longs enraptures all but the most heartless soul.

Longs has a tremendous east face, and its great sweep has struck emotion into the hearts of many. The emotions range from awe to terror. Longs' closest neighbor, Mount Meeker, has a huge, sweeping north face and, together, these two faces combine to form the greatest mountain cirque in Colorado. Nestled at the base of the east face of Longs is beautiful Chasm Lake. The east face of Longs and the north face of Meeker are separated by a large promontory called Ships Prow. Ships Prow rises directly above the south side of Chasm Lake to the Loft, which is the broad 13,450-foot saddle between Longs and Meeker.

The slabby north face of Longs rises above the Boulder Field. It is reached by the popular East Longs Peak Trail. The northwest ridge of Longs contains the famous Keyhole, which allows easy access from the east side of the peak to the west side. The large west face of Longs sweeps up out of Glacier Gorge and is bounded on the south by the well-named Keyboard of the Winds. The broken south side of the mountain rises above Wild Basin and contains the west-facing cliffs of the Palisades. The Notch is prominent on the ridge above the Palisades and is easily seen high above the east face of the peak.

Longs Peak has approximately 100 routes on it, but most of these routes are serious technical rock climbs on the great east face. Only a handful of the easier routes on Longs are included in this guide. Any route on Longs is a serious undertaking and should be treated as such. Somehow the

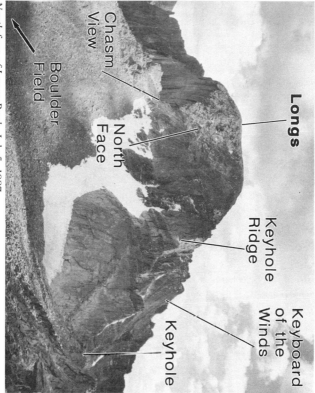

North face of Longs Peak. July 5, 1987.

Chasm
View

Boulder
Field

North
Face

Longs

Keyhole
Ridge

Keyboard
of the
Winds

Keyhole

popularity of the peak makes people feel safer. In fact, the opposite is the case. Many people believe that the greatest hazard in climbing today is being below other people.

Longs Peak is normally approached from the Longs Peak Trailhead. The East Longs Peak Trail leads to the Boulder Field at the base of the north face. The Boulder Field is on the popular Keyhole Route. A good spur trail leads from the East Longs Peak Trail to Chasm Lake at the base of the east face. It is 4.5 miles to Chasm Lake and 5.9 miles to the Boulder Field.

Keyhole II, Class 3, Moderate Snow in Early Summer * Classic *

This is the easiest route to the summit of Longs Peak. It must be the most popular route in Colorado, and it is climbed more than all the other routes in this guide combined. The experience of climbing the Keyhole Route on a late summer weekend is akin to walking on a crowded city sidewalk through a construction zone. Queues form on the Homestretch, one going up and the other going down. At midday, there can be more than 100 people on the summit. The Keyhole Route attracts several thousand people each summer.

This is a long and arduous ascent on a high and very real mountain. Many real people have died here. The difficulty of this route can increase dramatically when conditions are less than ideal. Storms can strike suddenly in the summer and turn the Homestretch into a bobsled run. The Trough usually contains snow until mid-July, and an ice axe is recommended until the snow melts out. The route spirals almost completely around the mountain, and any escape from the Keyhole Route takes you down into Wild Basin or Glacier Gorge. The return to the Longs Peak Trailhead from these drainages can assume epic proportions.

Even when conditions are good, the route is crowded, which does not make YOUR ascent safer. Stay true to yourself and the fundamentals of mountaineering. Don't be misled by someone else's energy on the mountain. It is always a good idea to check with a park ranger to get a report on current conditions before attempting an ascent.

From the Longs Peak Trailhead, follow the well-marked East Longs Peak Trail for 5.9 miles to the Boulder Field at 12,750 feet. Stay left at the Eugenia Mine/Storm Pass junction, left again at the Jims Grove junction and then right at the Chasm Lake junction. Do not go to Chasm Lake. From the Chasm Lake junction, the trail climbs to Granite Pass on the north side of Mount Lady Washington. Stay left at the North Longs Peak Trail junction in Granite Pass and continue southwest up into the expansive Boulder Field. The Boulder Field is below the slabby north face of Longs.

From the Boulder Field, continue southwest to the Keyhole, which is visible on the northwest ridge of Longs. The Keyhole is at 13,150 feet and consists of a large overhanging rock jutting out to the north. There is a small stone memorial building on the east side of the Keyhole. The Keyhole allows easy access from the east side of Longs to the west side. After scrambling up the rocks into the Keyhole, a great view of Glacier Gorge opens up before you. The route beyond the Keyhole becomes more serious and, if a retreat is indicated, this is a good place to turn around.

Scramble through the Keyhole to the west side of the ridge and traverse south on a series of ledges. The route beyond the Keyhole is marked with painted bull's-eyes on the rock, and it is hard to get lost. The route climbs to get above an area of west-facing, boiler-plate slabs, and there is a nifty V-slot in this section. After traversing across the top of the slabs, the route descends on the south side of the slabs. The route then climbs gently and reaches the large couloir called the Trough, 0.3 miles south of the Keyhole. The route gains very little elevation between the Keyhole and the Trough. This section of the route is exposed to the west wind, but the views of Glacier Gorge are excellent.

The Trough is a long couloir extending all the way from Glacier Gorge to a point high on the west side of Longs. Climb up the Trough from 13,300 feet to the top of the couloir on the west ridge of Longs at 13,850 feet. When the Trough has snow in it, try to avoid the snow by staying on the rocks north of the couloir. Just below the ridge at 13,850 feet, a chockstone must be passed. This may be the hardest move on the route. You can climb around either side of the chockstone.

On the platform at the top of the Trough you are close to the summit, but steep cliffs rise above you on both the west and south faces of the peak. A new vista to the south appears, and the route crosses to the south side of the peak. The route traverses east across the south face along a convenient ledge known as the Narrows. There is some exposure here but the ledge is wide.

Beyond the Narrows, continue east up ledges to the

base of the Homestretch. It is 250 yards from the top of the Trough to the bottom of the Homestretch. The Homestretch is the weakness in the summit cliffs, which the route has circled all the way around the peak to find. It consists of a series of parallel cracks angling up to the northeast across low angle slabs. The Homestretch is Class 3 when it is dry, but harder rock lurks nearby and care should be taken to stay in the cracks. People have gotten into trouble on the smooth slabs on either side of the cracks. After the Homestretch, the flat summit appears abruptly and the highest point is 100 feet north. The monarch is yours!

Variation

From the Glacier Gorge Trailhead, follow the Glacier Gorge Trail to Black Lake. Hike east and then south above the lake, get into the bottom of the Trough and ascend it to the west ridge at 13,850 feet. Follow the Keyhole Route to the summit. This is a good early-summer snow climb, which can provide more than 2,000 vertical feet of moderate snow.

When conditions are right, this is one of the longer snow climbs in the park. As summer progresses, so does the probability of rockfall from the large number of people climbing in or near the upper part of the Trough. By August, this is an undesirable route. The Glacier Gorge Trailhead is 200 vertical feet lower than the Longs Peak Trailhead, and this is a longer route than the Keyhole.

North Face II, Class 5.4

This is the old Cables Route which used to be the standard route up Longs. In 1973 the National Park Service

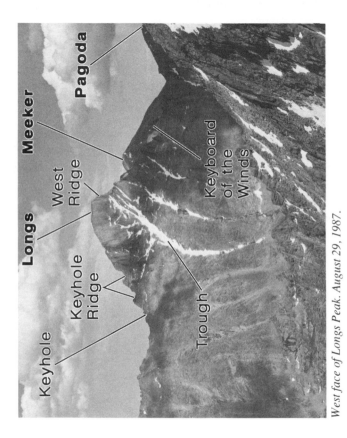

West face of Longs Peak. August 29, 1987.

removed the cables and this route reverted to its original difficulty. The eyebolts for some cables still remain and provide solid belay or rappel anchors. The route is most often used as a descent route. One 140-foot or two 70-foot rappels overcome the difficulties.

Follow the Keyhole Route to the Boulder Field. From the Boulder Field, hike south up to Chasm View, which is the notch just below the northeast edge of the north face. This vantage point offers an awesome view of the Diamond on the east face. From Chasm View, the route ascends a series of small, west-facing corners and slabs for one long or two short 5.4 pitches to reach easier ground. This is where the old cables used to be. Once you are above the slabs, follow the old, vaguely detectable trail up the talus field on the upper part of the north face to reach the summit.

Keyhole Ridge II, Class 5.5

This is an excellent technical route on Longs in a spectacular setting. The route ascends the northwest ridge of Longs. Some of the climbing is exposed, but it all works out. Follow the Keyhole Route to the Keyhole. Stay on the east side of the northwest ridge and ascend a Class 4 ramp for 200 yards to a higher notch in the ridge known as the False Keyhole.

Continue up the ridge past a gendarme, then follow a ledge on the west side of the ridge to a point below a steep face. Angle up across this face, crossing several ledges to regain the ridge. This face is the crux of the route. Any further difficulties can be passed on the west side of the ridge and, near the summit, you can stay right on the ridge. This route provides a unique approach to the huge summit plateau of Longs.

West Ridge II, Class 5.4

This route provides a fine technical finish to the Keyhole Route. Your ascent is bound to attract a lot of attention. Follow the Keyhole Route to the platform at 13,850 feet on the west ridge above the Trough. The route ascends the ridge above this point. Work up ledges and flake systems on the north side of the ridge for a pitch. Angle back up to the ridge crest in a tiny gully, then follow the ridge up past a small overhang. Continue up the ridge and pass a final steep section on the south side of the ridge. The climb requires three or four roped pitches.

Kieners III, Class 5.0–5.4, Moderate Snow/Ice
* Classic *

This is the finest mountaineering route on Longs Peak, and I believe that it is the finest mountaineering route in the park. The easiest route on the east face of Longs, it is a mixed climb involving both snow and rock climbing. Kieners is a serious undertaking and should not be tackled lightly. It is a difficult route to escape from. Once the rock above Broadway is engaged, the best retreat is a forward one over the top of the peak. This can be very difficult in bad weather.

From the Longs Peak Trailhead, follow the East Longs Peak Trail for 4.5 miles to the ranger cabin at Chasm Meadows below Chasm Lake. Scramble up a small gully directly west of the cabin to the east end of Chasm Lake at 11,800 feet. The view of the east face from here is world renowned.

East face of Longs Peak. June 14, 1987.

The upper part of the route can be seen from Chasm Lake and should be studied carefully. Broadway is the large ledge traversing completely across the face at half height. The vertical Diamond forms the upper, northern part of the face. The Notch can be seen on the skyline south of the summit. The Notch Couloir ascends from Broadway to the Notch. The upper part of Kieners ascends the broken face between the Notch Couloir and the Diamond. The Kieners Route is sometimes referred to as the Mountaineers Route.

Go west around the north side of Chasm Lake and continue west for another 0.25 miles toward the base of the great face. Mills Glacier is a permanent snowfield at the base of the lower face. Lambs Slide is a north-facing couloir connected to Mills Glacier, which ascends along the south side of the lower east face. Lambs Slide does not become visible until the bottom of the face is reached. There is permanent snow in Lambs Slide. It is prone to avalanching in early June and, as August progresses, it turns to ice.

The route ascends Lambs Slide to 13,000 feet where the multiple ledges of Broadway intersect Lambs Slide. Leave Lambs Slide, climb to the highest ledge and traverse north (right) along Broadway for 250 yards. The scrambling is easy initially, but the exposure increases rapidly as you traverse out over the lower face. Just as the exposure reaches a maximum, Broadway narrows and a delicate, Class 4 traverse must be made around a block. Many parties rope up at this point. A faux pas here could lead to a bad Broadway show.

The bottom of the Notch Couloir is a short distance north of the Class 4 block. The rock on the north side of the couloir must be reached, and this almost always requires crossing the snow or ice in the Notch Couloir. The Notch Couloir starts at Broadway above 800 feet of nearly vertical rock. The prospect of being flushed out of the couloir is something to carefully consider and avoid. This is an exciting place.

Do not get too high into the Notch Couloir before getting onto the rocks north of the couloir. The easiest line gets onto the rock 50 feet above Broadway. The rock is steep here but not as hard as it looks. Climb two 5.0–5.4 pitches to the broken upper part of Kieners Route. There are several ways to do this, and the easiest line is hard to find. Once you are on the broken, upper slopes of Kieners, scramble west up gullies and open slopes for several hundred feet. When this section of the face is dry, the difficulty does not exceed Class 4.

There are several steep cliffs at the top of this broken section of the face that bar easy access to the summit. The route traverses north (right) below these cliffs to reach a spectacular point at the top of the Diamond. This traverse is not obvious, but it is only Class 3. From the stance at the top of the Diamond, steep talus leads up to the summit. The flat summit provides an abrupt change of scenery.

Notch Couloir III, Class 5.0–5.2, Steep Snow/Ice * Classic *

When it is in good condition, this is the most spectacular snow climb in the park. The Notch Couloir ascends from Broadway to the Notch on the east face of Longs. It is in the best condition from mid-June to mid-July. By August, this couloir is melted out and no longer provides a viable climb. Conditions vary greatly in this couloir, and the route should be studied carefully before an ascent is undertaken.

Follow the Kieners Route to the bottom of the Notch Couloir. Ascend the couloir as it twists up the face to the Notch. The couloir is not consistent in its steepness and there are short, steep sections along the way. There are several places where you can escape north (right) onto the upper part of the Kieners Route. The angle in the couloir eases as the Notch is approached, and it is best to continue all the way into the Notch.

From the Notch, climb north up Class 3 ledges for 150 feet then ascend an east-facing chimney to the ridge above. This 5.0–5.2 chimney is 100 feet high. Once you are on the ridge, the difficulty eases considerably. Scramble north along the ridge for 100 yards to the summit. This is a dramatic approach to the flat summit of Longs.

Loft II, Class 3, Moderate Snow in Early Summer
* Classic *

In August, when the snow slopes have melted, this route is only slightly harder than the Keyhole Route. It is also shorter than the Keyhole Route and much less traveled. This route allows both Longs and Meeker to be climbed together. The Loft Route ascends the broad trough between Ships Prow and Mount Meeker to the Loft, then skirts below the west side of the Palisades to the Homestretch. When the ledges below the Loft are covered with snow, this route becomes dangerous. By August, the route becomes a Class 3 scramble.

From the Longs Peak Trailhead, follow the East Longs Peak Trail for 4.5 miles to Chasm Meadows below Chasm Lake. There is an old stone cabin here, but it is locked unless a ranger is in residence. From Chasm Meadows, do not go to Chasm Lake but hike straight south toward the huge, sweeping north face of Meeker. Once you are past the bottom part of Ships Prow, turn southwest (right) and ascend the wide slope between Ships Prow and the north face of Meeker. In June and part of July, this trough is filled with a moderate snow slope. The slope narrows, and simple passage to the Loft is blocked by a large, sweeping cliff band.

Scramble up 100 feet of broken, Class 3 rock to the base of the cliff band. Turn south (left) and get on a 10-foot-wide ledge angling up to the south across the cliff band. This ledge must be found if an easy ascent is to take place. Follow the ledge for 150 yards until it dies out into the broken, upper part of the cliff band (Class 3). Switchback north on a two-foot-wide, grass-covered ledge for 100 feet and scramble up to the talus below the Loft (Class 3). From the switchback point, you can climb straight up, but this is more difficult.

Cross the large expanse of the Loft to its northwestern edge. Contour northwest and look sharp for some cairns. Descend slightly and find the top of a gully leading down to the scree-filled couloirs on the south side of Longs. Traverse into the gully and scramble down for 100 feet to Clark's Arrow (Class 3). Clark's Arrow is an old painted arrow pointing south. It is on a smooth, west-facing slab just north of the bottom of the gully. It is visible for a long distance when descending from Longs to the Loft. It is not visible until you come right to it when using this route to ascend Longs.

Cairns lead you to the top of the descent gully, but the easiest route through this tricky section is actually 100 feet lower. When contouring northwest from the Loft, descend into a larger gully farther south. Leave this gully, angle northwest on some ledges and arrive easily at Clark's Arrow from the south.

From Clark's Arrow, scramble north and descend slightly to get below the cliffs of the Palisades. The Palisades are the beautiful, west-facing slabs that soar above you. The total elevation loss from the Loft to the low point below the Palisades is 150 vertical feet.

From the low point below the Palisades, the route becomes simpler. Scramble north up the scree-filled couloir below the Palisades. There is some loose rock in this couloir and you should be careful if there are other people on the route. At 13,600 feet, the couloir broadens out and easy ascent directly upward is blocked by the upper south face of Longs. The Notch is prominent up to the east.

Do an ascending traverse northwest (left) on some Class 3 ledges for 200 yards to join the Keyhole Route at 13,900 feet just below the Homestretch and follow that route to the summit. On the ascending traverse from 13,600 feet to 13,900 feet, you are below the Homestretch and should be on the lookout for falling objects.

Variation

At 13,600 feet, turn east (right) instead of west (left) and climb up into the Notch. This requires 30 feet of 5.0–5.2 climbing just below the Notch. Once you are into the Notch, finish the climb by following the upper part of the Notch

Couloir Route (5.0-5.2). This variation provides a technical finish to the already interesting Loft Route and avoids the crowds of the Homestretch.

Extra Credit

From the Loft, the summit of Meeker is a short hike up to the southeast.

Keplinger's Couloir II, Class 3, Moderate Snow in Early Summer

This is an easy route up the south side of Longs, but it is not usually climbed in one day because of the long approach and the 5,900 vertical feet of elevation gain. This route is best done with a camp at Sandbeach Lake or in cross-country zone 1G. With a high camp, the route provides a nice alternative to the crowded Keyhole Route.

From the Copeland Lake Trailhead at 8,350 feet, follow the Sandbeach Lake Trail to Sandbeach Lake at 10,283 feet. From the north end of the lake, head north and then west into upper Hunter Creek and find a small unnamed lake at 11,200 feet. Head north from the unnamed lake into the high basin formed by Meeker, Longs and Pagoda.

There are a number of couloirs and gullies on the south side of Longs. All of these couloirs reach the west side of the Palisades and, ultimately, the Notch. The Palisades are west-facing cliffs high on the southeast side of Longs. The Notch separates the Palisades from the summit of Longs. Keplinger's Couloir is the westernmost large couloir heading up toward the west side of the Notch. It has snow in it through June.

Follow the couloir to its end at 13,600 feet below the final summit cliffs on the south face of Longs. From this area, the Notch is prominent up to the east and the route is joined by the Loft Route. Do not head up to the Notch, but turn west (left) and angle northwest up ledges to join the Keyhole Route at 13,900 feet. This section of the route is below the Homestretch and rockfall is a possibility. Once you are on the Keyhole Route, continue up the Homestretch to the summit.

MOUNT MEEKER 13,911 feet

Meeker is the second highest peak in Rocky Mountain National Park and is 0.75 miles southeast of Longs Peak. When viewing Longs from the Denver metropolitan area, it is mostly the south and east slopes of Mount Meeker that are visible, with the summit of Longs just showing above Meeker.

Meeker is a wonderful peak with exciting mountaineering routes, but it is often overlooked because of its proximity to the much more famous Longs Peak. This should not be so. You can use the mountains as a testing place by simply zooming in and knocking off the big ones. A deeper knowledge and understanding of the mountain environment comes when you visit the lesser summits as well.

Meeker has VAST east, south and west slopes which are mostly covered with large talus blocks. Standing in sharp contrast to these gentle slopes is Meeker's sweeping

north face. The steepness and size of this face are apparent
from Meeker's pinpoint, exposed summit. This is one of the
larger faces in the park, but is really just a continuation of the
great east face of Longs. Together, these two faces combine
to form the greatest mountain cirque in Colorado.

The two faces are separated by a large promontory
called Ships Prow. Ships Prow rises directly above the south
side of Chasm Lake to the Loft, which is the broad 13,450-
foot saddle between Longs and Meeker. Meeker also has a
13,840+-foot false summit 300 yards east of the main
summit. The ridge between the false summit and the main
summit is narrow and exposed.

Most of the routes on Meeker start with a hike to Chasm
Lake. From the Longs Peak Trailhead, follow the East
Longs Peak Trail for 4.5 miles to the ranger cabin below
Chasm Lake. Take the southern (left) trail at the Eugenia
Mine/Storm Pass junction, the Jims Grove junction and the
Mills Moraine junction. The ranger cabin is in Chasm
Meadows at 11,600 feet and is locked unless a ranger is in
residence. Chasm Lake is 200 yards west of the cabin at
11,800 feet and can be reached by scrambling up the gully
directly west of the cabin.

Flying Dutchman II, Class 3–5.4, Steep Snow/Ice

This couloir is on the north face of Ships Prow and ends
at the north side of the Loft. There are a number of alterna-
tives from the Loft, but this couloir is included as a route on
Meeker. Flying Dutchman couloir is east of Lambs Slide.
Glacier Ridge separates the two couloirs.

Flying Dutchman is a long climb with an elevation gain

of 1,600 vertical feet from Chasm Lake to the Loft. It is a more difficult climb than Lambs Slide. In June, you can climb all the way from Chasm Lake to the Loft on snow and ice. In July, a rock gap appears at the crux. The upper part of the route, including the crux, is visible from the trail as you approach Chasm Meadows.

From Chasm Meadows, scramble west to Chasm Lake and hike around the north side of the lake. From the west end of the lake, the lower part of the couloir is visible to the south. Start into the wide couloir and climb up for a long distance on gradually steepening, moderate snow. The couloir narrows as it turns slightly west (right) and the crux becomes visible.

The crux is a 50-foot-high, eight-foot-wide steep section. On my June 14 ascent, this section was solid ice at a 55-degree angle. The water running underneath the ice spoke of its temporary nature and by July the ice was replaced by a rock pitch. Above the crux, the angle eases and the snow returns. The top part of Lambs Slide is 300 feet above the crux, and the northern edge of the Loft is another 150 feet southeast. The summit of Meeker is a short hike up to the southeast from the Loft.

Loft II, Class 3, Moderate Snow in Early Summer

This is the quickest way to reach the summit of Meeker from Chasm Meadows. It is often used as a descent route. The route ascends the wide slope between Ships Prow and Meeker to the Loft. When the ledges below the Loft are covered with snow, this route is dangerous. By August, the route becomes a Class 3 scramble. Follow the Loft Route on

North face of Mount Meeker. June 14, 1987.

Iron Gates

E. Summit

Dream Weaver

Meeker

Flying Buttress

Loft

Longs Peak to the Loft at 13,450 feet. From the Loft, the summit of Meeker is a short hike up to the southeast.

Dream Weaver III, Class 4–5.6, Steep Snow/Ice
* Classic *

Dream Weaver ascends a narrow couloir directly up the center of the sweeping north face of Meeker. When it is in good condition, this is one of the finest mountaineering routes in the park. The concave north face of Meeker has two large promontories protruding from it. The smaller, eastern one, the East Arete, should not be confused with the East Ridge. The larger, western one is a beautiful sweep of rock appropriately named the Flying Buttress. The Flying Buttress ascends directly toward the main summit of Meeker. The summit of the Flying Buttress is halfway up the face.

The Dream Weaver couloir starts on the east side of the Flying Buttress, then continues above the Flying Buttress to within 300 vertical feet of the summit of Meeker. The Dream Weaver couloir is only three feet wide in places, and it is difficult to see the entire route from a single vantage point. The lower and upper portions of the route can be seen from the trail as it approaches Chasm Meadows.

The nature of this climb varies a great deal depending on conditions. Parties have tried it in the winter expecting an ice climb, only to discover no snow or ice in the couloir at all. In early June, you can climb on snow from Chasm Meadows to the summit of Meeker. As summer progresses, the middle portion of the route melts out, generating a nice mixed climb. The upper portion of the couloir retains snow and ice through the summer. Crampons are recommended on this route in any season. Dream Weaver can appear quite intimidating at first, but just keep going. It all works out!

From Chasm Meadows, do not go to Chasm Lake, but hike straight south toward the huge, sweeping north face of Meeker. Do not vary to the right or left, but climb up to the base of the Flying Buttress at 12,500 feet. The first several hundred feet on the east side of the Flying Buttress are on a wide, moderate snow slope. The snow is almost always there.

The couloir abruptly narrows and steepens above the initial slope. In early June, there are 100 feet of steep snow before the angle moderates. By mid-July, this section has melted out to reveal an ugly chimney with two chockstones in it. The first chockstone is 5.4 and the larger, upper one is 5.6. While casting about in the dripping cave below the second chockstone, you might wonder if the dream has become a nightmare! Take heart as the angle moderates above this section.

Above the chockstones, ascend several hundred feet of moderate snow to reach a prominent notch between the summit of the Flying Buttress and the upper part of the north face. When this section is snow free, it requires 200 feet of 5.0–5.2 rock, which moderates to Class 2 scree as the notch is approached. You can escape from Dream Weaver at this notch by descending west from the notch down the basin on the west side of the Flying Buttress.

The best part of the route is above the notch, and the first half of the upper part is visible from the notch. Scramble up above the notch and enter the upper couloir. Thirty feet wide at first, the couloir relentlessly narrows and steepens. Three hundred feet above the notch, the essence of the dream will be yours. The couloir narrows to three feet and reaches 55 degrees. The couloir becomes a veritable ribbon of snow and ice reaching for the sky. With the Flying Buttress soaring beneath my front points, I am reminded of what started me climbing in the first place.

Above the initial ribbon, the couloir widens and moderates slightly for 100 feet before reaching a second crux. Sequels are never as good, and this second crux is not quite as enjoyable as the ribbon. Above the second crux, the couloir again widens and moderates slightly before reaching a final steep section. When this section is snow filled, a direct finish up the couloir is feasible. As the section melts out, it becomes preferable to climb a clean, solid 5.0–5.2 rock pitch on the west (right) side of the couloir.

The couloir deposits you on low-angle slabs 300 vertical feet below the main summit of Meeker. The easiest route to the summit continues up Class 3 gullies above the couloir to reach the summit ridge a short distance east of the summit. A harder alternative is to climb up large blocks and slabs west of the gullies to arrive directly on the summit. As you perch on the summit boulder of Meeker and look down your dream, you will be surrounded by a grand vista.

East Ridge II, Class 3

This is an easy route on Meeker that provides some spectacular views of Longs. The route is Class 2 up to the false summit, but then the narrow ridge to the main summit must be traversed. This ridge is a Class 3 scramble when dry, but it is exposed and difficult to escape from. It can be a very exciting place during a thunderstorm.

From Chasm Meadows do not go to Chasm Lake, but hike straight south toward the sweeping north face of Meeker. Turn east (left) and hike up a large talus field. Stay below all the cliffs on the north face of Meeker. Once you are east of these cliffs, turn south (right) and hike up talus to reach the east ridge at 12,900 feet. There are spectacular views of Longs Peak from this area. Hike southwest up the ridge on large talus blocks to reach the false summit at 13,840+ feet. The main summit is now visible 300 yards west, and this can be a sobering view for the unprepared.

Scramble west along the ridge toward the main summit. Near the low point between the summits there is a large block on the ridge with a small keyhole in it. This block is best passed on its north side and can be dangerous when there is snow on the ledges. Beyond this block, pick your way through a series of large boulders to reach the tippy top. The last Class 3 move up onto the summit boulder is exposed and exciting. Combining the East Ridge with the Loft Route makes a nice Tour de Meeker.

Variation

Iron Gates (Class 3). This is an interesting, scenic alternative between Chasm Lake and the upper part of the East Ridge. Instead of staying below all the cliffs on the north face of Meeker, ascend a west-facing trough between two buttresses at the eastern edge of Meeker's north face. This trough is talus lower down and involves some easy Class 3 scrambling as it approaches a notch in the east ridge at 13,000 feet. The trough narrows near the top as it becomes inset between the astonishing cliffs of the flanking buttresses. The view of Longs from here is outstanding.

South Ridge II, Class 2

This is the easiest route to the summit of Meeker. It is seldom ascended in one day because of its long and uninspired nature. Since this route starts at the Copeland Lake Trailhead, it requires an elevation gain of 5,600 feet compared to 4,500 feet for the routes that start at the Longs Peak Trailhead.

From the Copeland Lake Trailhead, follow the Sandbeach Lake Trail for 4 miles to Sandbeach Lake at 10,283 feet. From the lake, hike 1 mile south and work up onto the broad south slopes of Meeker. Eventually get onto the south ridge and ascend it directly to the main summit. There are a few cliffs on this ridge, but they can be avoided by staying away from the crest of the ridge.

9 WILD BASIN

This chapter covers the peaks on or east of the Continental Divide from Mount Alice to Buchanan Pass. Buchanan Pass is 4 miles south of the southern boundary to Rocky Mountain National Park. With one exception, the peaks in this chapter all rise at the headwaters of Wild Basin. Four thirteeners are covered in this chapter. The following U.S.G.S. quadrangles cover this area: Isolation Peak and Allenspark.

The peaks of Wild Basin are not as rugged as the peaks in Glacier Gorge or Longs Peak, but they provide a less-crowded experience. These peaks are approached on maintained trails from the Wild Basin Trailhead. The approaches are long, and the longest climbs in this book are in this chapter. Many blistered feet have limped home from Wild Basin. There is a price that must be paid for isolation!

MOUNT ALICE 13,310 feet

Mount Alice is a huge peak on the Continental Divide at the northwest end of Wild Basin. Alice has a stunning east face and a large, broken north face. The southwest side of the mountain is a vast talus slope extending all the way down to Spirit Lake on the west side of the divide. Mount Alice is quite remote and is a difficult peak to see. The best views of Alice are available in the backcountry. When Alice is visible, its distinctive shape is enticing.

Good trails approach Mount Alice from both the east and west sides of the divide. From the east side, the Thunder Lake Trail or the Lion Lake Trail can be used. From the west side, the East Inlet Trail is useable. It is a long hike to Alice, and this summit is reserved for those who persevere.

Hourglass Ridge II, Class 3 * Classic *

This is the north ridge of Alice, and it provides a sporting ascent between the peak's two great faces. This ridge also allows Chiefs Head and Alice to be climbed together. The approach to the base of this ridge is 8 miles long and is a hefty day climb.

From the Wild Basin Trailhead, follow the Thunder Lake Trail to its junction with the Lion Lake Trail. Follow the Lion Lake Trail northwest for another 1.5 miles to the first Lion Lake at 11,060 feet. Continue northwest past the second Lion Lake to Snowbank Lake at 11,521 feet. Continue northwest for another mile and hike up a faint trail to the broad saddle between Chiefs Head and Alice at 12,450 feet.

Hourglass Ridge is now visible to the south. The ridge starts out easily but soon becomes very narrow. Some exposed Class 3 scrambling is required to pass this narrow section. At 12,500 feet, the ridge broadens into a steep talus slope. Follow this up to the summit. The Class 3 scrambling on the narrow section is minimal, and it is reasonable to descend Hourglass Ridge.

South Slopes II, Class 2

This is the easiest route to the summit of Mount Alice. It is a long hike that presents no technical difficulties. It requires 19 miles round-trip from the east, 22 miles from the west and 4,900 vertical feet of elevation gain either way.

From the Wild Basin Trailhead, follow the Thunder Lake Trail to Thunder Lake at 10,574 feet. Continue west on a rough trail for another 1.5 miles to Boulder–Grand Pass at 12,061 feet.

Boulder–Grand Pass can also be reached from the west by starting at the East Inlet Trailhead and following the East Inlet Trail for 6.9 miles to Lake Verna. Continue east on a rough, unmaintained trail past the north sides of Lake Verna and Spirit Lake to Fourth Lake. From the north side of Fourth Lake, a faint trail climbs northwest then west to Boulder–Grand Pass.

From Boulder–Grand Pass, turn north and ascend the easy south slope of Alice for 1.1 miles to the summit. Persevere. Alice waits for you.

PILOT MOUNTAIN 12,200+ feet

This small summit is really just a spur of Mount Alice. Pilot Mountain is 0.6 miles southeast of Mount Alice and is part of a rugged cirque wall 0.6 miles northeast of Boulder–Grand Pass. This is a difficult summit to reach. Pilot Mountain can only muster two closed contours on the map, but it has a dramatic south face. This pilot clearly needs a navigator.

Descent

Descend the Northeast Face and Northwest Ridge Route.

Northeast Face and Northwest Ridge II, Class 4

This is the easiest route on Pilot Mountain. Predictably, it sneaks around the back side of the mountain. Follow the Hourglass Ridge Route on Mount Alice to the first Lion Lake at 11,060 feet. From here, hike west across open country for a mile to the small northeast face of Pilot Mountain. Climb west to the small saddle between Pilot Mountain and the slopes of Mount Alice (Class 3). This saddle is only 150 yards from the summit. Scramble southeast along the ridge toward the summit. The crest of the ridge becomes more difficult as the summit is approached. Avoid these difficulties by traversing on the north side of the ridge before climbing up to the summit (Class 4).

Variation

You can also traverse on the south side of the final summit ridge before climbing up a gully to the summit (Class 4). This traverse is more exposed than the north side traverse, but it provides a good alternative when the north side of the ridge is snow covered.

TANIMA PEAK 12,420 feet

The linear summit of Tanima is on a ridge jutting east from the Continental Divide. Tanima is 1.4 miles south of

Mount Alice and 1.5 miles northeast of Isolation Peak. Tanima rests in the shadow of these grand neighbors.

West Slopes II, Class 2

Tanima is easy to climb. Follow the South Slopes Route on Mount Alice to Boulder–Grand Pass. The summit of Tanima is 0.6 miles southeast across talus.

East Ridge II, Class 3

This is a more sporting route up the long east ridge of Tanima. From the Wild Basin Trailhead, follow the Thunder Lake Trail to Thunder Lake at 10,574 feet. The lower part of Tanima's east ridge is reached by bushwhacking south from the east end of Thunder Lake. Scramble west along the ridge for a mile to the summit.

Extra Credit

I have always liked crossing passes at right angles to ordinary, minimal east-west encounters. For a north-south crossing of Boulder–Grand Pass, ascend the east ridge of Tanima, descend to Boulder–Grand Pass, continue up to Alice and. . . . Let your condition and the spirit of the mountains guide you from there.

CLEAVER 12,200+ feet

This cunning pinnacle is on the Continental Divide 0.5 miles south of Boulder–Grand Pass. It can be approached from there or by following the Thunder Lake Trail to 10,400 feet and bushwhacking west for 2 miles to Indigo Pond.

Southeast Face II, Class 3

Cleaver is ascended by working up exposed ledges on its southeast face. If the easiest route is found, the difficulty does not exceed Class 3. Do not underestimate Cleaver. It has already produced a fatal accident.

Extra Credit

It is reasonable to combine an ascent of Cleaver with the North Ridge of Isolation Peak.

EAGLES BEAK 12,200 feet

This bantam beak peak perches deep in the heart of Wild Basin. It is 0.4 miles east of the Continental Divide and 1 mile northeast of Isolation Peak. Eagles Beak has a little east face and, if it were closer to a road, this would be a very popular peak. Untamed souls like it where it is.

Approach Eagles Beak from the Wild Basin Trailhead. Follow the Thunder Lake Trail to 10,400 feet, leave the trail and bushwhack southwest for a mile to Eagle Lake at 10,800 feet. Eagles Beak is 0.9 miles west of here and can be approached by working up benches and large ledges.

Southwest Face II, Class 3

This is the easiest route on Eagles Beak. Climb north from the northwest corner of Frigid Lake, then work back east (right) via ledges and small gullies to the summit.

East Face II, Class 4 * Classic *

The 600-foot-high east face of Eagles Beak offers a variety of wee adventures. You can ascend the east face and keep the difficulty at the Class 4 level. To do this, make judicious traverses on ledges and find the easiest places to move up. More difficult variations can be added to suit. This is a fun mountaineering route.

ISOLATION PEAK 13,118 feet

This well-named peak reigns supreme, far from the prying eyes of civilization. It is on the Continental Divide at the farthest reaches of Wild Basin. Isolation is a large peak that dominates a huge area as it overlooks several drainages. Most of Isolation's slopes are gentle, and this timeless peak is easy to climb. It does have a steep, broken north face rising above the headwaters of the East Inlet drainage on the west side of the divide. The southwest side of the peak drains into Paradise Park, and the east slopes drain into the various creeks of Wild Basin.

Isolation Peak can be approached from either the east or the west. The eastern approach is easier and gives access to the North Ridge and Southeast Slopes routes. From the Wild Basin Trailhead, follow the Thunder Lake Trail for 3.3 miles to its junction with the Bluebird Lake Trail. The choice of trail from here depends on the route.

From the west side of the divide, start at the East Inlet Trailhead and follow the East Inlet Trail for 6.9 miles to Lake Verna. Continue east for another 1.5 miles to Fourth

Lake. This approach gives access to the North Ridge, the North Face and the West Ridge routes.

North Ridge II, Class 5.0–5.2

This ridge is seldom climbed. The approach is long, and the climbing sections are short and of dubious quality. The north ridge of Isolation is one of the serious obstacles to hiking right along the crest of the Continental Divide. This ridge does provide a unique approach to the summit of Isolation.

This ridge can be approached from either the east or the west. From the east side of the divide, either continue west from Thunder Lake to Boulder–Grand Pass or follow the Thunder Lake Trail to 10,400 feet, leave the trail and bushwhack 2 miles west to Indigo Pond. From the west side of the divide, climb up the rough trail above Fourth Lake to Boulder–Grand Pass. From Boulder–Grand Pass, hike south, skirt the Cleaver on its east side then climb west to the Cleaver–Isolation col. From Indigo Pond, climb directly to this col.

From the Cleaver–Isolation col, the crux of the north ridge is apparent. The initial, northeast-facing cliff is bypassed on its west side (5.0–5.2). Easier climbing leads to a 300-yard traverse above large cliffs on either side of the divide. The major difficulties end at 12,800 feet. The rest of the ridge to the summit is an interesting 0.6-mile walk punctuated with some Class 3 scrambling.

North Face II, Class 4, Steep Snow

This route is seldom in condition for safe climbing.

This is usually a moot point since the approach to this climb is so long that few climbers worry about conditions on this face. The route ascends a long, east-angling ramp across the north face, which is prone to avalanching. After the snow melts, this ramp is rubble covered and undesirable. The first week in July on a good snow year is probably optimal for this route.

Hike around the west end of Fourth Lake and follow a very faint trail southeast up to Fifth Lake. The route up the face is visible from here and should be studied carefully. Head up a large couloir near the center of the north face and breach the lower cliffs. This couloir leads to the long, east-angling ramp. Follow it east (left) to the north ridge at 12,950 feet. Scramble 250 yards southwest to the summit. If you decide not to climb the north face after studying it from Fifth Lake, the west ridge is available as a safer alternative.

West Ridge II, Class 4 * Classic *

This is a good route for those determined to climb Isolation from the west side of the divide. It requires 23 miles round-trip and 5,000 feet of elevation gain. It is even a long day from a camp at Lake Verna. You will be rewarded with wilderness and isolation.

Hike around the west end of Fourth Lake and follow a very faint trail southeast up to Fifth Lake. This is one of the most pristine places in Rocky Mountain National Park. Climb southwest from Fifth Lake for 0.8 miles up steep grass and benches to the 11,900-foot saddle at the west end of Isolation's west ridge.

North face of Isolation Peak from Fifth Lake. August 10, 1987.

Ascend the west ridge for a mile to the summit. The ridge is easy initially, but three blunt towers must be crossed as the summit is approached. Some of the maneuvers in and out of the notches between the towers require a little Class 4 climbing.

The west ridge can be descended. A longer, easier descent can be done by dropping down Isolation's southwest slope and traversing west then north under the cliffs of the west ridge to regain the 11,900-foot saddle. This descent makes a long day even longer. You might as well descend to the east and complete a grand Tour de Isolation!

Southeast Slopes II, Class 2

This is the easiest route to the summit of Isolation. It is the most-used route on the peak and it is just a long hike. From the Wild Basin Trailhead, follow the Thunder Lake Trail for 3.3 miles, then follow the Bluebird Lake Trail for another 3.0 miles to Bluebird Lake. From here, hike west for a mile to Pipit Lake, then climb northwest for a final mile, passing Isolation Lake en route to the summit.

Extra Credit

Descend to the Isolation–Mahana col and ascend the west slopes of Mahana Peak (12,632 feet).

OUZEL PEAK 12,716 feet

This is a small summit on the Continental Divide, 1.2 miles south of Isolation and 1.1 miles north of Ogalalla.

Ouzel is not easily seen and rests in splendid obscurity between the headwaters of Wild Basin and Paradise Park. The summit of Ouzel can be reached by hiking along the Continental Divide from either the north or the south. Ouzel is often climbed together with Isolation or Ogalalla.

North Slopes II, Class 2

The easiest way to reach the Continental Divide near the summit of Ouzel is to follow the Southeast Slopes Route on Isolation Peak to Pipit Lake, then scramble up the north slopes of Ouzel.

Variation

This route can be made more difficult and interesting by following Ouzel's northeast ridge above Bluebird Lake. Any difficulties on this ridge can be bypassed on the north side of the ridge.

COPELAND MOUNTAIN 13,176 feet

This large mountain is 1.3 miles east of the Continental Divide, in the heart of Wild Basin. The south and northeast sides of the mountain are large talus slopes, which block the view of the divide to the west. The north face of Copeland is steep and broken, and it does not offer any coherent mountaineering routes. Copeland has a long, jagged west ridge which connects it to the Continental Divide midway between Ouzel and Ogalalla. This ridge is tower ridden and does not provide a reasonable route.

Northeast Slopes II, Class 2

The summit of Copeland is a long hike via its northeast slopes above Ouzel Lake. From the Wild Basin Trailhead, follow the Thunder Lake Trail for 3.3 miles, then follow the Bluebird Lake Trail for another 1.5 miles to Ouzel Lake. Hike south from Ouzel Lake, bushwhacking through downed trees to treeline, then head southeast for a long mile up talus to the summit.

Southeast Slopes II, Class 2

Copeland can also be climbed from Pear Lake. To reach Pear Lake, start at the Finch Lake Trailhead and follow the Finch Lake Trail for 4.6 miles to Finch Lake. Continue west for another 2 miles to Pear Lake.

The southeast slopes of Copeland above Pear Lake contain a series of cliffs. There are several ways to deal with them. For the easiest route and one that avoids all the cliffs, hike north from Pear Lake for 0.6 miles, then west for 1.2 miles to the summit.

ELK TOOTH 12,848 feet

This craggy peak is 0.7 miles east of the Continental Divide on the ridge that forms the southern boundary of Wild Basin. The north and south faces of Elk Tooth are steep and convoluted, especially the south face. Elk Tooth is a fun peak to climb and is not as hard as it looks. Elk Tooth is connected to Ogalalla on the Continental Divide by an interesting ridge. These two peaks are often climbed together. For a description of the connecting ridge, see the East Ridge Route on Ogalalla Peak.

East Ridge II, Class 3

This is the easiest route to the summit of Elk Tooth. The route can be approached from either Wild Basin or the Middle Saint Vrain drainage. The Wild Basin approach is longer and requires more elevation gain. Follow the Southeast Slopes Route on Mount Copeland to Pear Lake. From here, hike southwest then west for 1.3 miles to Hutcheson Lakes at 11,200 feet. From here, turn south (left) and climb to a shoulder on the east ridge of Elk Tooth at 12,100 feet.

The length of the approach from the Middle Saint Vrain Trailhead depends on how far you drive up the 4WD road in the lower part of the valley. From the valley, hike west up the Saint Vrain Glacier Trail to 10,800 feet, then climb northwest to the 12,100-foot shoulder on the east ridge of Elk Tooth.

From the shoulder, climb west up the ridge to 12,600 feet where the ridge flattens out. Continue west on or near the ridge crest. Any difficulties can be avoided by staying on the north side of the ridge. As the summit is approached, the ridge opens onto a talus slope and the summit is easily reached from the northeast.

OGALALLA PEAK 13,138 feet

This important peak is on the Continental Divide at the southwest corner of Wild Basin and the northwest corner of the Middle Saint Vrain drainage. The long east ridge of

Ogalalla, which includes Elk Tooth, separates Wild Basin from the Middle Saint Vrain drainage. A long ridge running west from Point 13,049 feet just south of Ogalalla separates Paradise Park from Hell Canyon and the Roaring Fork.

After the southern park boundary was changed to follow the Paradise Park–Hell Canyon ridge line, Ogalalla became the southernmost thirteener in Rocky Mountain National Park. Ogalalla is the highest summit on the Continental Divide for 5 miles to the north and 10 miles to the south!

Ogalalla is a rugged, challenging and rewarding peak. All of the approaches to Ogalalla are long. Because of its remote position, it is not climbed very often. It can be approached via Wild Basin, Middle Saint Vrain or Hell Canyon. The Middle Saint Vrain is the most used and shortest approach. Once you are on the Continental Divide, the summit of Ogalalla can be reached by hiking. The trick is getting up on the divide. Several routes can help you with this process.

Cony Pass II, Class 4

This is the easiest route from Wild Basin to the Continental Divide near the summit of Ogalalla Peak. It is not a good descent route. The easiest descent route to Wild Basin is to traverse north to Ouzel Peak and descend the North Slopes Route on that peak.

Cony Pass is not a pass on the Continental Divide, but a pass on the ridge connecting the Continental Divide with Copeland Mountain. Cony Pass, at 12,200 feet, is 300 yards east of the divide and 350 vertical feet below it. To reach it, follow either of the approaches described with Copeland

Cony Pass from the south. August 10, 1987. Cony Pass is in the center of the photo, and the southern Cony Express is on the left.

Mountain and continue west toward the Continental Divide.

Cony Pass is most easily reached from Cony Lake to the south, but can also be reached from Junco Lake to the north. Either way requires scrambling up steep scree with some minor Class 3 scrambling. From Cony Pass, climb west near the steep ridge to the divide (Class 4). A difficult buttress on the north side of the ridge can be avoided by staying on or south of the ridge. Once you are on the divide, the summit of Ogalalla is a 0.5 mile stroll south.

Cony Express II, Class 3, Steep Snow

There are two snow couloirs that reach the Continental Divide near Cony Pass. Either of these steep couloirs offers a challenging route up Ogalalla. The couloirs are difficult to see as they are hidden by Mount Copeland. The narrower and steeper couloir is 300 yards southwest of Cony Pass and the other couloir is 250 yards northwest of the pass. Good snow remains in these couloirs until mid-August.

Refer to the Cony Pass Route for the approaches to either Junco Lake or Cony Lake. For the southern couloir, hike to Cony Lake. For the northern couloir, hike to Junco Lake. The couloirs are obvious and easily reached from their respective lakes. The ascents of the couloirs are steep, but there are no serious cornices above the couloirs.

It is difficult to see both couloirs during the approach. If you are not sure which couloir to climb, it is best to hike to Cony Lake. If you don't like the southern couloir, then scramble up to Cony Pass. You can reach the upper part of the northern couloir by traversing west on the north side of the ridge above Cony Pass. If you don't like the northern couloir, then retreat to Cony Pass and continue up the Cony Pass Route. Once you are on the divide, the summit of Ogalalla is 0.5 miles south.

East Ridge II, Class 4 * Classic *

This is the connecting ridge between Ogalalla and Elk Tooth, a rugged peak to the east of Ogalalla. The connecting ridge is 0.7 miles long and is a wonderful scramble that allows both Elk Tooth and Ogalalla to be climbed together. The ridge requires route-finding but is not as hard as it looks. Any Class 4 climbing encountered is minimal and short. The climb can be executed from either Wild Basin or the Middle Saint Vrain. See Elk Tooth for those approaches.

From the summit of Elk Tooth, descend northwest on talus and stay on the north side of the ridge. As the Elk Tooth–Ogalalla col is approached, there are several towers that must be bypassed. Take your time and don't rush into anything difficult. With a little looking around, surprise ledges can be found to get around these towers.

From the Elk Tooth–Ogalalla col, move to the south side of the ridge and climb west toward Ogalalla. The scrambling for several hundred feet above the col does not exceed Class 2. As Ogalalla is approached, the climbing becomes more difficult. A final, southeast-facing cliff guards the summit of Ogalalla. Stay on the south side of the ridge. Traverse southwest on ledges under the final cliff, then climb north up a gully to the summit (Class 4). An alternative finish is to climb the southeast (right) side of the final cliff (Class 4) and approach the summit from the east.

Ogalalla Peak from the south. August 10, 1987. Ogalalla Express is below the shadowed face, and the East Ridge is to the right of the summit.

Ogalalla Express II, Class 3, Moderate Snow

This is the easiest route up Ogalalla from the upper Middle Saint Vrain drainage. It is also a good descent route. It ascends a long, narrow scree slope on the south side of Ogalalla which reaches the Continental Divide 200 yards southwest of the summit. This slope has some moderate snow on it through July, but by August the snow is gone. This is not a very pleasant route once the snow has melted.

From the Middle Saint Vrain Trailhead, hike up the Saint Vrain Glacier Trail to 10,900 feet. Continue west under the south face of Elk Tooth to the base of the southeast face of Ogalalla at 12,000 feet. This point is between the northernmost Saint Vrain Glacier and Ogalalla. The route is visible to the west.

The route ascends either of a pair of southeast-facing scree ramps right under the broken south face of Ogalalla. Seek out or avoid any snow as you see fit. The upper part of the scree ramps run into some small cliffs below the divide, and some Class 3 scrambling and/or moderate snow climbing is required to reach the divide. The exact route through these minor cliffs is a matter of choice. There are several small couloirs running up through the final cliffs, and these couloirs retain snow longer than the lower part of the route. The route reaches the divide in the broad saddle between Point 13,049 feet and Ogalalla. The summit of Ogalalla is a 200-yard stroll up to the northeast.

Southwest Slopes II, Class 2

This is the easiest route up Ogalalla from the west side of the divide. It is a long hike and is normally done with a high camp in upper Hell Canyon at either Stone Lake or Upper Lake. The route can also be reached from a camp at Gourd Lake. Upper Hell Canyon can be reached via the Hell Canyon Trail or the Roaring Fork Trail. The Roaring Fork Trail is the easier and preferred approach. Gourd Lake is reached via the Cascade, Buchanan Pass and Gourd Lake trails.

From Upper Lake in Hell Canyon, climb east up scree and talus to the 11,850-foot saddle between Cooper Peak and a long slope leading north up to the Continental Divide. This saddle can be reached from Gourd Lake by hiking north to Island Lake at 11,400 feet, then northwest up a scree slope for 0.4 miles to the saddle. This is a pristine and beautiful area.

From the saddle north of Cooper Peak, climb north for 0.6 miles up to the Continental Divide. This slope is steep at first but gradually relents. Go over the summit of Point 12,945 feet, alias "Ooh La La!" There is a good view from this summit of Ogalalla and Elk Tooth. Ooh La La!

Descend northwest from the summit of "Ooh La La!" on talus and climb north to Point 13,049 feet. This stretch of the Continental Divide can look a bit imposing but, with a little route-finding, the difficulty is only Class 2. On the summit of Point 13,049 feet, you enter Rocky Mountain National Park and, for a moment, you can stand suspended between the splendors of the Indian Peaks Wilderness and the park. The summit of Ogalalla is a gentle 0.4-mile stroll northeast, and it eagerly awaits you.

"OOH LA LA!" 12,945 feet

This unnamed peak is on the Continental Divide 0.6 miles south of Ogalalla Peak. "Ooh La La!" is at the west end of the Middle Saint Vrain drainage. It is a significant summit with a steep northeast face rising above the northernmost Saint Vrain Glacier. In fact, "Ooh La La!" directs the entire chorus of Saint Vrain Glaciers flowing below it.

"Ooh La La!" is usually climbed together with Ogalalla and ascended as part of the Southwest Slopes Route on Ogalalla. It is easily approached from the southeast by hiking along the Continental Divide. There are some interesting mountaineering routes on the east side of the peak.

Ooh La La Express II, Class 3, Steep Snow * Classic *

This route ascends the northernmost and largest Saint Vrain Glacier, and the nifty, twisty couloir above it. This couloir reaches the Continental Divide in the col between "Ooh La La!" and Point 13,049 feet. There is snow in this couloir year round.

Follow the approach for the Ogalalla Express Route on Ogalalla to 11,800 feet in the high basin between Ogalalla and "Ooh La La!" From here, climb southwest and ascend the large, northern Saint Vrain Glacier. The angle of the glacier is moderate. The steep, express couloir is above the top of the glacier on the north side of the northeast face of "Ooh La La!"

By August, a large bergschrund forms between the couloir and the glacier. This bergschrund can prove to be a significant problem in late summer. The couloir turns south

"Ooh La La!" from the north. August 10, 1987. Vrain Drain is just left of center. "Ooh La La" is just right of center, and Ooh La La Express is on the far right.

before it reaches the divide and, as the couloir is inset into the face, a helmet is recommended for this climb. There is not a serious cornice problem at the top of the couloir, and once you are on the divide, the summit of "Ooh La La!" is 250 yards southeast.

Vrain Drain II, Class 3, Steep Snow

This couloir rises above the Saint Vrain Glacier just south of "Ooh La La!" It reaches the Continental Divide 0.3 miles south of the summit of "Ooh La La!" There is snow in the couloir year-round, but a gap begins to form near the top in August.

Follow the approach for the Ogalalla Express Route on Ogalalla to 11,400 feet then head southwest to the bottom of the glacier. This glacier is smaller and steeper than the northernmost Saint Vrain Glacier. It sweeps up to the obvious, steep couloir above it.

In August, there is a bergschrund between the glacier and the couloir, but you can avoid it. This couloir is not inset into the face and is really just an upper arm of the glacier. Any cornice at the top of the couloir is very blunted by August and can be easily bypassed on the rocks north of the couloir in any case. Once you are on the divide, the summit of "Ooh La La!" is a 0.3-mile stroll north.

10 West Side of the Park

This chapter covers all of the high peaks in the park on the west side of the Continental Divide. The following U.S.G.S. quadrangles cover this area: Grand Lake, McHenrys Peak, Shadow Mountain and Isolation Peak. There are only seven peaks in this chapter, but they are important ones. These peaks hide far away from the crowds that swarm on the eastern side of the divide. For example, fewer people climb Nakai in 10 years than climb Longs Peak in one summer day! If it's solitude that you are looking for, then these peaks are for you.

These peaks are best done with a high camp, and that fact enhances the experience. The peaks provide a chance to return to fundamentals: sunrise, sunset, frost in the morning, a bull elk strolling past your camp, the phases of the moon and your favorite constellation. These are things that we often do not take time for on our mad dashes into the mountains in the pursuit of SUCCESS. How ironic. These are the very experiences that moved most of us to go into the mountains in the first place!

In many ways, this is the only essential chapter in this book. I finished climbing every peak in Rocky Mountain National Park 10 years ago. I was SUCCESSFUL. Ten years later, that success seemed unimportant. When I returned to the summit of Nakai in preparation for this chapter,

I remembered why I started. That experience has been much more important.

NAKAI PEAK 12,216 feet

This reclusive peak is 1.2 miles southwest of the Continental Divide in the middle of nowhere. Nakai stands between Onahu Creek to the north and Tonahutu Creek to the south. Hardened east-side peak baggers can find relief from the "I've seen it all blues" on the slopes of Nakai. This is a good area to see deer and elk. Large herds of elk sometimes congregate on the open slopes southeast of the summit.

The approach to Nakai is long, but it is on good trails. From the Green Mountain Trailhead, follow the Green Mountain Trail east for 1.8 miles to Big Meadows and the Tonahutu Creek Trail. Follow the Tonahutu Creek Trail north, then east for another 5.1 miles to 10,400 feet and the sign for the Haynach Lakes Campsites. This point is 200 yards east of the creek descending from Haynach Lakes. Leave the Tonahutu Creek Trail, follow a good spur trail steeply northwest, pass the two Haynach Lakes Campsites at 10,700 feet and continue northwest on the spur trail to Haynach Lakes at 11,060 feet.

Nakai Peak is a long day hike from the trailhead, but it is short from a camp at Haynach Lakes. The total distance from the trailhead to Haynach Lakes is 8.3 miles, with an elevation gain of 2,260 feet.

Elk near Haynach Lakes Campsite. August 15, 1987.

Northeast Ridge II, Class 2

This route is long, but it is the easiest route on Nakai. It is a 19-mile round-trip from the trailhead. From Haynach Lakes, climb northwest for 0.5 miles to the 11,600 feet saddle between Nakai and the Continental Divide. From the saddle, climb southwest for 0.7 miles over Point 12,052 feet to the summit of Nakai. There is some steep talus below Point 12,052 feet.

East Face II, Class 3 * Classic *

This route is slightly shorter than the Northeast Ridge and adds a little scrambling to the adventure. From Haynach Lakes, hike southwest then west to the base of the east face and ascend it directly to the summit. The east face averages 35 degrees for 600 vertical feet and is quite broken. A little jocular route-finding takes you up from ledge to ledge. Ascending the East Face Route and descending the Northeast Ridge Route makes a nice Tour de Nakai.

SNOWDRIFT PEAK 12,274 feet

This peak is 2.9 miles west of Flattop Mountain on the Continental Divide and 2.8 miles southeast of Nakai Peak. The gentle summit area of Snowdrift Peak is above some rough country. The south side of the peak rises 3,000 vertical feet above the North Inlet, and the north side rises 2,000 feet above Tonahutu Creek. The northeast ridge of Snowdrift connects with Bighorn Flats near Sprague Pass on the Continental Divide.

Snowdrift is most easily approached from 11,600 feet on the Tonahutu Creek Trail as it crosses Bighorn Flats. This point is 8.8 miles from the Green Mountain Trailhead and 7.2 miles from Bear Lake. Snowdrift makes a wonderful day climb from a camp in upper Tonahutu Creek. If you are determined to climb Snowdrift in one day, then go for it from Bear Lake.

Northeast Ridge II, Class 2

This is the easiest route on Snowdrift. From 11,600 feet on the Tonahutu Creek Trail, contour southwest for 0.7 miles to the 11,550-foot saddle between Snowdrift and the open slopes of Bighorn Flats. From the saddle, continue southwest up the ridge for another 0.7 miles to a bench east of the summit. Point 11,933 feet can be bagged en route or skirted on its north side. A major elk migration route crosses the bench east of the summit. From the bench, climb west up rough talus for 300 yards to the summit.

Variation

A more difficult approach to Snowdrift is up Ptarmigan Creek southeast of the peak. The hike from the North Inlet Trail to Bench Lake is one of the rougher half-miles around, but it gives access to the pristine basin north of Bench Lake. Ptarmigan Creek is the park's cross-country zone 2M and, if you can get your pack up here, this is a wonderful place to camp. This basin is full of deer and elk.

To reach Bench Lake, start at the North Inlet Trailhead. Follow the North Inlet Trail for 6.0 miles to 9,300 feet where Ptarmigan Creek descends from Bench Lake. Fifty yards east of the creek, leave the security of the North Inlet Trail and follow a faint trail northeast into the heart of the wilderness. This "trail" stays on the east side of the creek and climbs steeply past the cascades of War Dance Falls to Bench Lake. The trail degenerates to an occasionally cairned route as the falls are approached. Some Class 3 scrambling is required to get past the falls.

From Bench Lake, hike north up Ptarmigan Creek through a trailless fairyland for 1.5 miles to a beautiful unnamed lake at 11,060 feet. From the unnamed lake, climb north up a moderate scree slope to the 11,550-foot saddle between Snowdrift Peak and Bighorn Flats. Continue on the Northeast Ridge Route to the summit.

PTARMIGAN MOUNTAIN 12,324 feet

This secluded summit is at the west end of a long ridge running west from Mount Alice. This major ridge separates the North Inlet drainage to the north from the East Inlet drainage to the south. The south and west sides of Ptarmigan Mountain are gentle, but the north and east sides are steep. The salient feature of Ptarmigan Mountain is the five, east-facing "Ptarmigan Towers" rising above Lake Nanita. These towers have become increasingly popular with rock climbers in recent years. Ptarmigan Mountain is also spectacular when viewed from Lake Nokoni.

Ptarmigan Mountain offers a variety of interesting routes, and can be approached from either the North Inlet or

"Ptarmigan Towers" from Lake Nanita. August 13, 1987. Tower Five is on the left, and Tower One is on the right.

the East Inlet. From the North Inlet Trailhead, follow the North Inlet Trail for 9.9 miles to Lake Nokoni. From the East Inlet Trailhead, follow the East Inlet Trail for 5.5 miles to Lone Pine Lake.

Ptarmigan Mountain makes a nice day climb from a high camp in either the North Inlet or the East Inlet. Camping is not permitted at either Lake Nokoni or Lake Nanita, but there are several designated camping sites lower down on the North Inlet Trail. There are also several designated camping sites near Lone Pine Lake. For a one-day ascent of Ptarmigan Mountain, use the South Slopes Route.

Northeast Ridge II, Class 2

This is the easiest route up Ptarmigan Mountain. The approach is long but on a good trail. From the north side of Lake Nokoni, follow game trails north for 300 yards to the 11,200-foot saddle between Point 11,322 feet and Point 11,733 feet. This saddle is used when hiking between Lake Nokoni and Pettingell Lake. From the saddle, hike southwest up the ridge for 0.3 miles to Point 11,733 feet and descend southwest from Point 11,733 feet to the broad, open slopes on the northwest side of Ptarmigan Mountain. Hike southeast up these slopes for 0.4 miles, then head east for 200 yards to the highest point. A tombstonelike slab of rock is propped up near the summit cairn.

East Ridge II, Class 3 * Classic *

This is a sporting route that flirts with the back sides of the "Ptarmigan Towers." There is only a little Class 3 scrambling but lots of excitement. The broad east ridge separates Lake Nokoni from Lake Nanita. The towers are on the Lake Nanita side of the ridge.

From Lake Nokoni, continue south for 0.3 miles on the main trail to the 11,060-foot saddle between Lake Nokoni and Lake Nanita. Leave the trail, hike southwest and ascend the wide slope west of the "Ptarmigan Towers." The towers are not easily distinguished at first, but as the slope is ascended their summits can be seen. Tower One is the lowest, and Tower Five is the highest. There is a huge gap between Tower Three and Tower Four, which frames Longs Peak. This is a spectacular place, and there is a lot of air around here.

Continue up on the west side of all the towers to a small col between Tower Five and the summit slopes of Ptarmigan Mountain. Scramble northwest above this col to a small notch in the narrow east ridge. This notch is 50 yards east of the final summit cliff of Ptarmigan Mountain, and the rest of the route is visible from here. Do an ascending traverse west for 50 yards on the north side of the ridge to another notch directly under the summit cliff (Class 3). Scramble north for 80 feet and ascend a 30-foot-high, south-facing Class 3 slot to the summit plateau. The highest point is 200 yards west.

Extra Credit

The summits of the "Ptarmigan Towers" provide short climbs on their west sides and can be ascended for extra excitement. The views from these summits are excellent and, if you are lucky, a golden eagle will come soaring up between the towers to check you out. Tower One is Class

5.4, Tower Two is Class 4, Tower Three is Class 3, Tower Four is Class 4 and Tower Five is Class 3. Whew!

South Slopes II, Class 2

This is the shortest route on Ptarmigan Mountain. It involves a scruffy bushwhack and is not as easy as the Northeast Ridge Route. The South Slopes Route is approached via the East Inlet Trail and is the route to use when climbing Ptarmigan Mountain together with Andrews Peak. The ridge between these two peaks is 2 miles long, but is just a hike.

From Lone Pine Lake, bushwhack northwest to treeline and get on a rounded spur ridge. Climb north up this ridge to the gentle slopes near the top of Ptarmigan Mountain. Continue north to the highest point.

ANDREWS PEAK 12,565 feet

This important peak is the highest summit on the long ridge running west from Mount Alice. This major ridge separates the North Inlet drainage to the north from the East Inlet drainage to the south. Andrews Peak is 1.5 miles southeast of Ptarmigan Mountain and 2.5 miles west of Mount Alice. Andrews has steep north and east faces, but the rest of the peak is gentle. The summit of Andrews has the distinction of carrying the best summit cairn in the park. It's not the largest, just the best. It is a work of art.

Southeast Couloir II, Class 3, Moderate Snow
* Classic *

This is the easiest route on the east side of Andrews. This couloir reaches the 11,860-foot saddle, 0.4 miles south of the summit. This saddle separates Andrews from the 12,241-foot summit of "Ptarmigans Beak," 0.5 miles southeast of the saddle. The couloir holds moderate snow through mid-July, but in August the couloir is a scree gully.

The approaches to this wilderness couloir are long. This route is likely to be climbed only from a high camp and is reserved for the dedicated backcountry traveler. There are two approaches that can be used. From the North Inlet Trailhead, follow the North Inlet Trail for 9.9 miles to Lake Nokoni and continue on the trail for another mile to Lake Nanita. Hike southeast around the east side of Lake Nanita and continue southeast on a disappearing trail for another mile to an 11,400-foot saddle east of Andrews. Descend south from this saddle to the start of the route.

For the second approach, start at the East Inlet Trailhead and follow the East Inlet Trail for 7.5 miles to Spirit Lake. Bushwhack north to the 11,400-foot saddle between "Ptarmigans Beak" and Mount Alice. This is a difficult bushwhack. Descend northwest from the saddle to a small unnamed lake at 11,100 feet and continue descending northwest to the start of the route. The last part of this descent is over huge boulders under the steep northeast face of "Ptarmigans Beak."

The route starts by climbing southwest up grass-filled Class 3 cracks on smooth slabs to the basin between Andrews and "Ptarmigans Beak." After the snow melts out, this basin is full of condo-sized boulders, and crossing the basin to the base of the couloir is a time-consuming task. The couloir rises 300 vertical feet from the southwest end of this small basin to the saddle between Andrews and "Ptarmigans Beak." After the snow melts out, this couloir is still a viable route. From the saddle, the summit of Andrews is 0.4 miles north up talus.

South Slopes II, Class 2

This is the easiest route on Andrews Peak. It is an arduous hike with some off-trail bushwhacking. From the East Inlet Trailhead, follow the East Inlet Trail for 6.9 miles to Lake Verna. From the west end of Lake Verna, continue on the trail along the north side of the lake for 300 yards. The introduction is over. Leave the trail and bushwhack north up the steep slope to treeline at 11,000 feet. This is a difficult bushwhack, but once you reach treeline, life improves. Continue north up talus for a final mile to the summit of Andrews.

"PTARMIGANS BEAK" 12,241 feet

This significant, unnamed peak is 0.8 miles southeast of Andrews Peak and 2.0 miles west of Mount Alice. It rises at least 361 vertical feet from the saddle connecting it to Andrews. "Ptarmigans Beak" sports a very steep, 1,000-foot-high northeast face. This is the largest steep wall west of the Continental Divide in Rocky Mountain National Park.

West Slopes II, Class 2

Climbing "Ptarmigans Beak" is almost a carbon copy of climbing Andrews Peak, and these two peaks are usually climbed together. Choose either of the routes given with Andrews. The summit of "Ptarmigans Beak" is 0.5 miles southeast across talus from the saddle at the top of the Southeast Couloir on Andrews. When using the South Slopes Route above Lake Verna, simply bear east from treeline to the summit of "Ptarmigans Beak." There is a great rocking boulder a few feet from the summit. Rock on!

MOUNT CRAIG 12,007 feet

This peak is the westernmost summit on a long ridge running west from Isolation Peak. This ridge separates the East Inlet drainage to the north from Paradise Park to the south. Mount Craig is the prominent peak visible to the east when hiking up the lower part of the East Inlet Trail.

The north slopes of the peak are steep. In 4,000 horizontal feet they rise more than 2,000 vertical feet above Lone Pine Lake! The gentler south slopes of Mount Craig rise above beautiful Ten Lake Park, which is on a bench north of Paradise Creek. Day hiking is permitted in Paradise Park, but camping is prohibited.

Northeast Bowl II, Class 3

This is the most practical route up Mount Craig, and it avoids the complications of hiking into Paradise Park. It is a rough scramble above Lake Verna, which is not feasible until after July 1. It is a reasonable day climb from the East Inlet Trailhead and a short day climb from a camp at Lake Verna.

Follow the East Inlet Trail for 6.9 miles to the west end of Lake Verna at 10,200 feet. Leave the trail, cross to the south side of the creek and bushwhack south up the steep slope into a basin under the north face of Mount Craig. Stay east of two north ridges and work up into the large upper basin between Mount Craig to the west and Point 11,959 feet to the east. Climb up talus to the saddle at 11,650 feet between Point 11,959 feet and Point 11,902 feet. Turn west, climb over Point 11,902 feet and continue west on easy terrain for 0.7 miles to the summit of Craig.

"FLEUR DE LIS" 12,250 feet

This significant, unnamed summit rises at least 330 vertical feet above its connecting saddle with Isolation Peak. "Fleur de Lis" is 1.5 miles east of Mount Craig and 1.5 miles west of Isolation Peak. It is the highest summit on the long ridge running west from Isolation Peak that separates the East Inlet drainage from Paradise Park.

"Fleur de Lis" is a rugged, off-trail hike that can be combined with Mount Craig, Isolation Peak or both. The summit area of this peak is gentle but there is a spectacular cirque on the north side of the peak. From the summit of "Fleur de Lis" you can look down on the flat summit of the sagacious "Aiguille de Fleur" rising above Spirit Lake. "Fleur de Lis" is a wonderful peak tucked away from the pressures of civilization. Yes, there is wilderness in Colorado.

West Slopes II, Class 3

This is the shortest route on "Fleur de Lis." Follow the Northeast Bowl Route on Mount Craig to the saddle at 11,650 feet between Point 11,959 feet and Point 11,902 feet. From this saddle, climb east on gentle slopes for 0.75 miles to the summit.

East Slopes II, Class 2

This is a longer, easier and very scenic route on "Fleur de Lis." Follow the West Ridge Route on Isolation Peak to the 11,900-foot saddle at the base of Isolation's west ridge. From this saddle, hike west across gentle slopes for 0.6 miles to the summit.

11 Special Events and Divide Traverses

The last chapter of this book is devoted to interesting ways that the peaks in this book can be climbed together. It is common in Colorado to climb two or more peaks together. The special events and traverses discussed here are arduous events that combine three, five, seven, 12 and even 30 peaks.

These events are for climbers who are looking for new ways to challenge themselves. All of these events are challenging. Some of the challenges can be accomplished in one day. Some of the events require several days and take on an expedition flavor.

Finally, this chapter covers several routes that cross the Continental Divide, as well as a lengthwise traverse of the divide. Traversing across or along the Continental Divide on foot is an interesting and challenging project. It spawns a pioneer spirit.

There is a lot of room for creativity when planning an excursion from one watershed to the other. You can go from east to west or from west to east. There are numerous places where crossings can be made. Some are easy and some are strenuous. A crossing can be done in one or more days.

Since the trailheads are generally higher on the east side of the divide, it is usually easier to start on the east side. While any crossing can be done in either direction, they are all given from east to west for consistency. They are also ordered from north to south. Obviously, any crossing of the divide requires a significant vehicle shuttle. It helps to be dropped off and/or picked up.

In addition to the events described in this chapter, some people may choose to challenge themselves by climbing all the classic routes in this book. Would someone like to set a speed record for that event? Since I just created this designation, I can announce that my record is 35 years! Certainly someone can do better than that.

After that, you can climb every peak in Rocky Mountain National Park. Don't forget to climb all the fourteeners in Colorado. Heck, why stop there? Climb every fourteener in the United States, Canada and Mexico, plus the 10 highest peaks in North America.

How about the 50 classic climbs in North America? For the soul who first achieves that feat, I can only hope that some diabolical author doesn't write a book called *Another Fifty Classics!* I can see it now. All of these successful people end up in Classic Climbers Heaven. They stroll into the library for a little look around and what do they find? Titles like: *Classics Galore!*, *More Classics!*, *More Classics Galore!*, *2,001 Colorado Classics!*, *My Life with the Classics!* Hell's library (with apologies to Gary Larson).

Say! How about Everest? Then there are the seven continent summits. Then there are all the 8,000-meter peaks. Anyone got a ticket to the moon? Mars?

Some people rely on the 10 essentials. I rely on my Classic Commandments of Mountaineering:

1.   Never get separated from your lunch.
2.   Never get separated from your sleeping bag.
3.   Never get separated from your primal urges.
4.   Carefully consider where your primal urges are leading you.
5.   One must go the wrong way at least some of the time.
6.   First aid above 26,000 feet consists of getting below 26,000 feet.
7.   Never step on the rope.
8.   Never bivouac.
9.   Surfer Girl is not in the mountains.
10. Never pass up a chance to pee.
11. Don't eat yellow snow.
12. Have fun and don't forget why you started.

Unmentionable Traverse (two to four days)

Once upon a time, a July trip to the Never Summer Mountains turned into winter camping practice when dawn revealed five inches of snow outside the tent! The Never Summer Mountains lived up to their name that day. Ever since then, the Never Summer Mountains have been referred to in hushed tones as "The Unmentionables." The lengthwise traverse of the Never Summer Mountains has been named in memory of that summer snowstorm.

There are several possible itineraries for a lengthwise traverse of the Never Summer Mountains. This section describes the longest traverse, with some shorter plans given as variations. These peaks are lined up on the Continental Divide just waiting for you to mow them all down! Get in shape before attempting this traverse!

Day 1. Three peaks, 10.5 miles, 3,730 vertical feet of elevation gain. Start at the Colorado River Trailhead on Trail Ridge Road. Head north along the Colorado River Trail to La Poudre Pass. Climb west over Mount Neota, Thunder Mountain and Lulu Mountain. Descend west to Thunder Pass and Michigan Lakes. Camping is allowed at Michigan Lakes with a permit from Colorado State Forest. For extra credit you can hike up Point 12,018 feet, alias "The Electrode," before dinner. There are no technical difficulties on this day.

Day 2. Five peaks, six miles, 3,500 vertical feet of elevation gain. Ascend the East Ridge Route on Static Peak, traverse to Mount Richthofen and get ready to point it down range. Traverse south over Tepee Mountain, Lead Mountain and Mount Cirrus. The Class 4 north ridge of Lead is the most difficult part of the entire traverse. Other portions of the ridge require some Class 3 scrambling.

From the Mount Cirrus–Howard Mountain col, descend to one of the designated campsites in Hitchens Gulch below Lake of the Clouds. This is a significant descent and you may wish to camp on the Continental Divide. Since the divide is the Rocky Mountain National Park boundary, it is legal to camp west of the ridge crest on national forest land, although water can be difficult to find.

Day 3. Five Peaks, seven miles, 4,600 vertical feet of elevation gain. Climb back up to the Cirrus–Howard col and continue south over Howard Mountain, Mount Cumulus, Mount Nimbus and Mount Stratus to Baker Mountain at the end of the ridge. This ridge is rough but non-technical. Descend west from Baker Mountain to the Baker Gulch

Trail and follow the spur trail west up to Parika Lake. This lake is in Routt National Forest and no camping permit is needed.

Day 4. Seven peaks, 16 miles, 3,800 vertical feet of elevation gain. Climb north to Point 12,253 feet, alias "Paprika Peak," and follow the Continental Divide south over Parika Peak, Farview Mountain, Point 12,442 feet, alias "Never Summer Peak," to Point 12,280+ feet. Take a side trip out to Bowen Mountain and back if desired. Descend southwest to Bowen Pass, continue south over Ruby and Point 12,198 feet, then climb Cascade Mountain. Descend to Bowen Lake and follow the Bowen Gulch Trail down to the Bowen/Baker Trailhead.

Escape

The traverse can be easily escaped by descending the South Slopes Route of Mount Cirrus to the Colorado River Trailhead.

Variations

1. Day one can be eliminated by starting at the Lake Agnes Trailhead and following the West Ridge Route on Richthofen. This version of the traverse requires a long vehicle shuttle but, when combined with Variation 2, reduces the traverse to the heart of the range.

2. Day four can be eliminated by following the Baker Gulch Trail down to the Bowen/Baker Trailhead.

3. Day four can be shortened by eliminating the ascent of Bowen Mountain and/or by descending the Bowen Gulch Trail from Bowen Pass.

Mummy Mania II, Class 3

This voyage collects all the mummies. It is a one-day traverse of the Mummy Range that nets you six peaks. It requires 16 miles and 5,600 vertical feet of elevation gain. It also requires two vehicles. Park one vehicle at the Lawn Lake Trailhead and drive the other up Fall River Road, which is one way up.

Start at the Chapin Pass Trailhead and climb the west slopes of Mount Chapin, Mount Chiquita and Ypsilon Mountain. Continue northeast to Fairchild. The traverse between Ypsilon and Fairchild requires some Class 3 scrambling and is the most difficult part of the traverse. The traverse from Fairchild to Hagues Peak is easy.

On top of Hagues, your peak-bagging energy is tested. Hard-core peak baggers head north from Hagues to climb Rowe Peak and Rowe Mountain. These two humble summits are over 13,000 feet. This addition adds 2 miles and 700 vertical feet to the adventure.

From the top of Hagues, do the easy traverse to Mummy Mountain. Descend the South Slopes Route on Mummy and follow the Lawn Lake Trail down to the Lawn Lake Trailhead. Retrieve vehicle one and drive back up Fall River Road to retrieve vehicle two. Both vehicles can then return to civilization via Trail Ridge Road.

Milner Pass to Bear Lake II, Class 3

This one-day traverse has proven popular over the years as a test piece for peak baggers. The route traverses south along the Continental Divide from Milner Pass to Flattop Mountain, then descends the Flattop Mountain Trail to Bear Lake. This traverse nets you seven peaks and possibly as many as 12. The traverse requires 17 miles, 4,500 vertical feet of elevation gain and 5,800 vertical feet of descent. The traverse is a good way to climb the obscure peaks, like Cracktop and Sprague, along this stretch of the divide. You need to arrange a vehicle shuttle between Milner Pass and Bear Lake.

Start at Milner Pass on Trail Ridge Road at 10,758 feet. Follow the North Ridge Route on Mount Ida and continue south along the divide across Chief Cheley Peak. Take the short side excursion to the summit of Cracktop. The descent of the southwest side of Ida, the south ridge of Chief Cheley and the final scramble to the summit of Cracktop all require a little Class 3 scrambling. These areas are the most difficult portions of the traverse.

From Cracktop, continue southeast near the divide for a long 2.5 miles to Sprague. The three unnamed points along this stretch of the divide can be summited or skirted on the west as you desire. Going over the tops of these points adds to the 4,500 vertical feet of gain and provides some good views. Somewhere between Cracktop and Sprague you pass the point of no return.

From Sprague Mountain, descend south for a mile to Sprague Pass, then head southeast across Bighorn Flats for 1.6 miles to Knobtop Mountain. Hobble south for 0.8 miles to Ptarmigan Point, descend south to the Tonahutu Creek Trail and follow it east for 0.7 miles to the summit of Flattop Mountain. For the downhill finale, follow the Flattop Mountain Trail for 4.4 blistering miles to Bear Lake.

Escape

From almost any point between Cracktop and Sprague Pass, you can descend west to the Tonahutu Creek Trail and follow it west to the Green Mountain Trailhead.

Variation

The finish of the traverse can be made slightly easier by getting on the Tonahutu Creek Trail 0.8 miles south of Sprague Pass at 11,800 feet. Follow the Tonahutu Creek Trail to the summit of Flattop Mountain as it skirts west of the summits of Knobtop and Ptarmigan Point.

Extra Credit

The following extra peaks can be added singly or combined in concert with your peak-bagging needs. Doing all five extra peaks turns this adventure into a Herculean day climb!

1. From the summit of Cracktop, climb northeast for 0.6 miles to the summit of Mount Julian and return to Cracktop (Class 3).

2. From 0.3 miles west of Sprague, follow the Continental Divide version of the Southeast Face and Northeast Ridge Route on Hayden Spire (Class 5.0–5.2). Return to the Continental Divide and carry on.

3. From Sprague Pass, march east for 1.5 miles to Gabletop Mountain, then head north for 0.7 miles to Knobtop (Class 2).

4. From Point 12,280+ feet between Knobtop and Ptarmigan Point, follow the Continental Divide variation of the Southeast Gully and Northwest Ridge Route on Notch-

top (Class 4). Return to the divide and carry on.

    5.   From the summit of Flattop Mountain, take a deep breath and climb south to Hallett Peak (Class 2). Return to Flattop and stagger down to Bear Lake.

Grand Slam III, Class 3   * Classic *

    This is a tough day climb that ascends Longs Peak and the four peaks surrounding it. The Grand Slam requires 16 miles and 7,300 vertical feet of elevation gain. The peaks are climbed in the following order: Mount Meeker, Longs Peak, Mount Pagoda, Storm Peak and Mount Lady Washington. This has been a popular peak-bagging test piece for years, and it has been done in 10 hours. The Grand Slam requires no vehicle shuttle as it starts and finishes at the Longs Peak Trailhead.

    Follow the Loft Route up Meeker and return to the Loft (Class 3). Continue on the Loft Route up Longs (Class 3). Descend the Homestretch and look sharp for a good place to descend west toward Pagoda. Do not go too far west towards the Narrows before dropping off. The descent to the 13,100-foot saddle between Longs and Pagoda requires some Class 3 scrambling. Climb the northeast ridge of Pagoda and return to the Longs-Pagoda saddle. The three hardest peaks have been climbed but the action is not yet over.

    Climb back up toward Longs to 13,400 feet in the Keyboard of the Winds. Descend a gully on the northwest side of the Keyboard of the Winds to 13,100 feet and traverse north to regain the Keyhole Route on Longs near the point where the Keyhole Route enters the Trough (Class 3). Follow the Keyhole Route north to the Keyhole (Class

3). Now it's all over but the marching.

From the Keyhole, ascend the Keyhole variation of the East Slopes Route on Storm and descend east to the Boulder Field. Climb the Northwest Slopes Route on Lady Washington and descend the East Slopes Route on Lady Washington to the East Longs Peak Trail. Go ahead, break the record. Sprint down to the trailhead!

Triple Crown III, Class 4

The point of this exercise is to climb McHenrys Peak, Chiefs Head Peak and Mount Alice in one day. These three peaks are above Glacier Gorge, Wild Basin and the North Inlet. The Triple Crown can be done from any of those three drainages. The Glacier Gorge approach requires 17 miles and 6,700 vertical feet of gain, while the Wild Basin approach requires 22 miles and 7,400 vertical feet of gain. The North Inlet approach is even longer and would only make sense with a high camp in the North Inlet. A high camp would make the climb easier from the other drainages as well.

From Glacier Gorge, follow the Stone Man Pass Route on McHenrys (Class 4) and return to Stone Man Pass. Continue on the Northwest Ridge Route up Chiefs Head and descend to the Chiefs Head-Alice saddle (Class 3). From here, ascend the Hourglass Ridge Route on Alice and return to the Chiefs Head-Alice saddle (Class 3). From here, climb northeast to 12,700 feet, rejoin the Northwest Ridge Route on Chiefs Head and descend it over Stone Man Pass back into Glacier Gorge (Class 3).

From Wild Basin, climb the Southeast Slopes Route on

Chiefs Head and descend the Northwest Ridge Route on Chiefs Head to Stone Man Pass (Class 3). Climb the Stone Man Pass Route up McHenrys and return to Stone Man Pass (Class 4). Retrace the Northwest Ridge Route on Chiefs Head to 12,700 feet and descend to the Chiefs Head-Alice saddle (Class 3). Climb the Hourglass Ridge Route on Alice (Class 3). Descend the South Slopes Route on Alice to Boulder–Grand Pass and descend east back into Wild Basin (Class 2).

From treeline in the North Inlet below Lake Powell, climb east past Lake Powell and reach Stone Man Pass from the west (Class 2). Ascend the Stone Man Pass Route up McHenrys and return to Stone Man Pass (Class 4). Continue on the Northwest Ridge Route up Chiefs Head and descend to the Chiefs Head-Alice saddle (Class 3). From here, climb the Hourglass Ridge Route on Alice (Class 3). Descend west and then northwest from the summit of Alice for 0.8 miles to a broad shoulder at 13,000 feet (Class 2). Descend north on steep but broken slopes for a mile back into the North Inlet (Class 2). Take a nap.

Terra Tomah Mountain–Nakai Peak II, Class 3
* Classic *

This challenging route across the divide is largely trailless. It is likely to be used by peak baggers trying to climb the obscure summits along the way. This traverse can be done in one day, allowing you to climb three to five remote peaks. These peaks are hard to reach by any route, and this traverse can be intensely rewarding. It requires 16 miles, 4,200 vertical feet of elevation gain and 7,100 vertical feet of descent. Because of its proximity to Trail Ridge Road, the vehicle shuttle for this traverse is shorter than any other.

Start at the Forest Canyon Overlook on Trail Ridge Road. Follow the Northwest Ridge Route on Terra Tomah Mountain (Class 3). From the summit of Terra Tomah Mountain, continue southwest over Mount Julian to Cracktop (Class 3). Scramble southwest from the summit of Cracktop to the Continental Divide (Class 3). Descend south to the 11,600-foot saddle between the Continental Divide and Nakai Peak. Climb the northeast ridge of Nakai (Class 2). Descend Nakai by either the Northeast Ridge Route (Class 2) or the East Face Route (Class 3) to Haynach Lakes and the Tonahutu Creek Trail. Follow the Tonahutu Creek Trail west for 5.1 miles to the Green Mountain Trail. Follow the Green Mountain Trail west for 1.8 miles to the Green Mountain Trailhead.

Variations

1. The traverse can be made slightly easier by descending southwest from the summit of Julian to 11,900 feet on the south side of the Julian–Cracktop Ridge, then climbing southwest to a 12,300-foot saddle on the Continental Divide. This variation avoids the Class 3 scrambling to the summit of Cracktop, but the elevation gain is the same.

2. The traverse can be made easier by not climbing Nakai. From the 11,600-foot saddle between the Continental Divide and Nakai, descend southeast to Haynach Lakes and the Tonahutu Creek Trail. Skipping Nakai decreases the elevation gain by 600 vertical feet.

Extra Credit

After climbing over Cracktop, scramble north along the Continental Divide to Chief Cheley (Class 3). Return south along the divide for 0.2 miles and rejoin the traverse route.

Flattop Mountain I, Class 1

This is the most popular divide crossing in Rocky Mountain National Park because it is entirely on established trails. It is a scenic tour that penetrates the heart of the park. It requires 16 miles, 2,850 vertical feet of elevation gain and 3,500 vertical feet of descent. It can be done in one long day, or more sedately with a camp in either Tonahutu Creek or the North Inlet on the west side of the divide.

Start at Bear Lake and follow the Flattop Mountain Trail for 4.4 miles to the summit of Flattop Mountain on the Continental Divide. Continue west for 0.25 miles to the trail junction between the Tonahutu Creek Trail and the North Inlet Trail.

The northern trail is the Tonahutu Creek Trail and this is the shortest route. Follow the Tonahutu Creek Trail west for 9.6 miles to the Green Mountain Trail and follow that trail west for 1.8 miles to the Green Mountain Trailhead.

Variation

From the trail junction near the summit of Flattop, take the southern trail which is the North Inlet Trail. This trail reaches the Tonahutu/North Inlet Trailhead after 12.6 miles. This route is 1.2 miles longer than the Tonahutu Creek Trail. In 1987 there was a typo on the trail sign at the west end of the North Inlet Trail. The sign claimed that Bear Lake was 16.3 miles from the Tonahutu/North Inlet Trailhead but in reality it is 17.3 miles.

Andrews Pass I, Class 2, Easy Snow

This traverse is slightly more difficult than the Flattop Mountain Traverse, but it is even more scenic and has the added excitement of crossing a glacier. It requires 15.5 miles, 2,800 vertical feet of elevation gain and 3,500 vertical feet of descent.

Start at the Glacier Gorge Trailhead and follow the Andrews Glacier Route on Otis Peak to Andrews Pass on the Continental Divide. Andrews Pass is at the top of the Andrews Glacier. Descend west for 0.5 miles on gentle slopes to the North Inlet Trail and follow that trail west for 10.8 miles to the Tonahutu/North Inlet Trailhead.

Extra Credit

From Andrews Pass, climb northeast for 0.5 miles to the summit of Otis Peak (12,486 feet).

Boulder–Grand Pass II, Class 2

This popular traverse is largely on maintained trails, as it spends much of its time deep in the valleys of Wild Basin and the East Inlet. It is a wonderful tour through magnificent country. It requires 17.5 miles, 3,550 vertical feet of elevation gain and 3,650 vertical feet of descent. This traverse works equally well in either direction.

Start at the Wild Basin Trailhead and follow the Thunder Lake Trail west for 6.8 miles to Thunder Lake. Continue west for another 1.5 miles on a rough trail past Lake of Many Winds, then climb to Boulder–Grand Pass at 12,061 feet. Descend west for a mile on a rough trail to the north side of Fourth Lake. Continue west on the improving trail along the north sides of Spirit Lake and Lake Verna. From Lake Verna, follow the East Inlet Trail west for 6.9 miles to the East Inlet Trailhead.

Pfiffner Traverse (one to two weeks) * Classic *

In the late 1950s, Carl Pfiffner spoke passionately about traversing from the Arapaho Peaks to Longs Peak along the Continental Divide. This project retains all of its original mystique and is the ultimate mountaineering adventure in the Front Range. The adventure can be extended by going from Berthoud Pass to Milner Pass. There are many variations to this complicated project, and any attempt requires your creativity. It certainly challenged mine. I have climbed in the Front Range for over 30 years, but this quest gave me a much deeper respect for it.

There are several technical obstacles to traversing right on the crest of the Continental Divide. From south to north they are: north ridge of Neva, southwest face of South Arapaho, northeast ridge of North Arapaho, north ridge of Deshawa, northwest ridge of Arikaree, north face of Navajo, north ridge of Apache, north ridge of Toll, northwest ridge of Paiute, north ridge of Isolation and McHenrys Notch. Overcoming all of these problems on one continuous journey is a monumental project indeed!

Dropping off the divide to avoid the tough spots leads to other problems. The drainages must then be crossed "against the grain," producing large elevation gains and losses. The trail system does not help much, as the trails generally follow the east-west drainages. Any traverse on or near the divide is a significant undertaking that is not done very often.

I had toyed with the idea of doing a trip along the divide since the 1950s, but the idea of carrying ropes and hardware for many miles along the easy stretches of the divide and then dangling on the tough spots with all the camping gear had deterred me for many years. Finally in 1987, my wife, Deirdre, and I did our own version of the Pfiffner Traverse. There are as many variations on this theme as there are people to do them so I include our plans and itinerary as a general guide for those who are interested in pursuing this grand adventure.

Our trip went from Berthoud Pass to Milner Pass because those are the two paved roads that bind the heart of the Front Range. We chose to go from south to north for no really good reason other than it seemed more aesthetic to march north. The trip took 16 days simply because that was the number of days we had to devote to the project. It was a two-week vacation. Our goal was not to stay on the crest of the divide exactly, but to move through interesting country, climb lots of peaks and be away from civilization for 16 days. We worked out a detailed schedule with 10 days for forward marching and six days for day climbs along the way.

Camping reservations were the next order of business. You cannot camp above treeline in Rocky Mountain National Park. This meant that we would have to drop down each night into a cross-country zone or a designated camp-site. Many areas of the Indian Peaks Wilderness are also on the designated campsite system as well. We went to Rocky Mountain National Park's backcountry office first and got reservations as close to the original plan as possible, then went to the U.S. Forest Service and got the rest of our reservations. Finally, to keep our packs from being too heavy, we carefully hid three food caches near Columbine Lake, Crater Lake and Lake Verna. This caching effort ultimately required 80 extra miles of hiking.

We started the traverse on August 1 after a night of tremendous thunderstorms. Here is our story.

Day 1. The trip started in a swirling mist punctuated by dawn. Climbing silently above Berthoud Pass, I looked north. I turned to Deirdre, pointed and said a single word: "Ida." It was only an outline and impossibly far away.

Forward march! We went from Berthoud Pass to Rogers Pass. We carried our packs over Colorado Mines Peak, Flora, Eva, Parry, Bancroft and James before drop-ping wearily down to Rogers Pass after 10 hours of effort. Our original plan called for dropping down to Heart Lake to camp, but it was a beautiful evening and we elected to camp right on the divide. It was our only chance to do so easily. We melted snow for water.

Day 2. Forward march! We went from Rogers Pass to Columbine Lake, crossing the entire East Portal Quadrangle in one swell foop. We summited many of the unnamed peaks along this stretch of the divide, including "Heart Beat Peak," "Sprint Peak" and "Skyscraper Peak." We also peered down every couloir as we strolled along in shorts and running shoes. Finally, running out of time and growing weary, we traversed on the west sides of Jasper and Neva. We descended the lower part of Neva's northwest ridge to Columbine Lake and our first food cache. This was another 10-hour day.

The logic behind covering so much ground in the first two days was simply to buy us more playtime in the heart of the range. We needed perfect weather for these two days and, fortunately, we got it. Our food cache kept our packs light. Even so, if I were going to do the trip again, I would allow three days for this distance.

Day 3. We went from Columbine Lake to the nice campsite at 9,840 feet on the Arapaho Pass Trail west of the divide. This was an easy day. We carried our packs over the top of Satanta Peak and descended the grass directly to Caribou Lake. This was a good shortcut.

Day 4. Our first day climb. We bushwhacked from the bridge on the Arapaho Pass Trail at 9,740 feet directly up to "Lost Tribe Lakes" and climbed the southwest face of "Iroquois," then traversed to "Hopi." The bushwhack up to the lakes was tough and convinced us to abandon plans for carrying our packs to Crater Lake via a high route that we had spotted earlier. From the top of "Hopi," we descended to Point 12,056 feet then dropped straight south down a steep avalanche chute that worked out well and deposited us on the Arapaho Pass Trail five minutes below camp.

Day 5. We hiked to Crater Lake on the Arapaho Pass and Cascade trails. Our decision to abandon the high route was a good one. The trail miles flowed by easily. We were learning. The goodies in our second food cache were great!

Day 6. Day climb time. We hurried up Lone Eagle Peak just minutes ahead of a serious storm, then beat a retreat back to the tent. We were entertained that evening by "Bugs," a friendly bunny near the tent.

Day 7. RAIN!! We had grand plans for our second day climb from Crater Lake, but they got washed up. We took a rest day. No sign of "Bugs" today.

Day 8. We hiked from Crater Lake to Island Lake. We followed the Cascade Trail, Buchanan Pass Trail and Gourd Lake Trail, then bushwhacked above Gourd Lake to the highest site we could find above Island Lake. We were slightly sick from the "slime-ing" that we received at Crater Lake, and this turned into a tough day. That evening we were treated to a young red fox who pranced around the tent trying to play with me as I lay in the tent with only my head sticking out. He came within a few feet of me and we played.

Day 9. We did a leisurely day climb of Cooper and Marten. I found my own name on Marten from 10 years earlier. We kept this day easy in preparation for the next one.

Day 10. This turned out to be our toughest day. We went from Island Lake to Lake Verna and in so doing crossed from the Indian Peaks Wilderness into Rocky Mountain National Park. The park does not allow camping in Paradise Park (a research natural area), and the closest legal campsite to the Indian Peaks Wilderness is at Lake Verna. Our original plan was to cross the 10,500-foot pass at the north end of Hell Canyon and work through Paradise Park near treeline. We wisely abandoned this plan and got back up on the divide. In this case the decision to go high was a good one.

The day began at dawn. Through the wind-swept morning we carried our packs over "Ooh La La!," Ogalalla and Ouzel, then dropped our packs near the 12,200-foot pass south of Isolation. After bagging Isolation from the south, we continued our Tour de Isolation by contouring around to the 11,900-foot pass on the west side of the peak. We had to drop lower than we wanted to avoid a section of house-sized boulders, then slogged wearily back up to the pass. We dropped our packs again and bagged "Fleur de Lis" before descending past Fifth Lake to finally reach our Lake Verna camp. This was an 11-hour day, and we again had perfect weather when we needed it. In spite of the goodies in our food cache, we were too tired to eat much. The Monarch Lake drainages had held us for seven nights, but we were in a new domain now.

Day 11. We spent the next morning reorganizing our third and final food cache. In the afternoon we went back up to Spirit Lake, then bushwhacked up to the 11,400-foot pass between "Ptarmigans Beak" and Mount Alice. This bush-whack was steep at first, but then moderated. We were learning to minimize these encounters. From the pass, we descended into the park's cross-country zone 3M. The East Inlet drainage had held us for only one night but it had been an intense time.

Day 12. Our original plan for this day was to do the Triple Crown, but the reality of bushwhacking up to Lake Powell, then getting out of that basin the next day, sank in along with a new bunch of clouds. We climbed Andrews

Peak and "Ptarmigans Beak" instead. As I watched the clouds move in on McHenrys Peak, I realized that McHenrys Notch had pushed us this far west.

Day 13. We went from zone 3M to zone 2M. We climbed to the 11,400-foot pass northeast of Andrews, then descended to Lake Nanita and picked up the trail. We had learned to use the trails when we could. We dropped our packs on the 11,050-foot pass between Lake Nanita and Lake Nokoni then climbed Ptarmigan Mountain via the east ridge behind the "Ptarmigan Towers." On the descent we scrambled up to the top of Tower Three and were treated to a huge golden eagle that spiraled up between the towers to check us out.

We zoomed down the trail into the depths of the North Inlet, then cast about in the rain for a trail up to Bench Lake. We found a vaguely cairned route as we struggled up past the cascades of War Dance Falls. This was the toughest bushwhack of the trip, but at least our camp would be legal. We went beyond Bench Lake to camp at the edge of a huge meadow full of deer that seemed unconcerned with our existence. This had been a tough day, but we were getting hardened to the routine.

Day 14. We floated up the pristine basin of Ptarmigan Creek and surprised several elk. We dropped our packs on the 11,550-foot pass at the head of the basin and climbed Snowdrift Peak. I remembered standing on this summit with Bruce Carson in May 1975. Bruce had transmitted a real love of the mountains on that trip. He died later that summer in the Himalayas when a cornice broke under him.

The North Inlet had held us for three nights. Back at our

packs, we rolled north and picked up the Tonahutu Creek Trail, which led us easily to our designated campsite below Haynach Lakes. An icy wind had blown all day. The heat wave was over. An entire herd of elk including a bull with a huge rack wandered within feet of our tent all night. This was their territory and we felt like intruders.

Day 15. Our final day climb. We went back up the Tonahutu Creek Trail and fought upward in a blasting wind to the top of Sprague Mountain. We could only look at Hayden Spire, as the wind was strong enough to knock us over. Hayden Spire had been my last peak in Rocky Mountain National Park almost 10 years earlier, and I had hoped to revisit that summit.

Day 16. Our final day began at midnight with rain drumming steadily on the tent. The weather had gone "out." Our final day was planned to be one of those exposed days when we needed to spend many hours on the divide. As I lay in the tent, I desperately wanted to finish the traverse and wondered just how bad it would have to be to keep us off the divide. The rain continued to fall, and the clouds gripped our tiny tent. How many nights had I lain awake on the great peaks of the world willing the clouds to part and the wind to fall? This trip had taken on an expedition flavor.

We started moving at dawn. We spread out the maps and, with the headlight on, worked out all the alternate routes. They were not good. We either went high or we bailed out. The rain stopped and we moved up. As we ascended so did the clouds, and we could see new snow on the divide. We dropped our packs on the 11,600-foot pass above Haynach Lakes and headed for Nakai. Chief Cheley and Ida were still socked in. As we climbed, the clouds parted. They were being torn apart by our old friend the wind. On the summit of Nakai, I remembered my other visit to this summit 12 years earlier. It was a moment out of time.

While we climbed Nakai, the snow was melting on the divide. It was still August. We made our final big push upward and went out to Cracktop. I peered intently down the Cracktop Couloir. We scrambled over Chief Cheley and faced the peak that had seemed impossibly far away on that first morning. Ida was our 30th peak. On the summit a mangy marmot was cruising around and intently sniffing the wind. He was sniffing for winter. We rolled down.

As we approached Milner Pass, a tourist asked me, "Where does this trail go?" Without breaking stride I replied, "Berthoud Pass! . . . but you have to walk for 16 days!"

We came. We saw. We climbed. The only thing we left behind was the following nonsense in a summit register somewhere between Berthoud Pass and Milner Pass.

> *'Twas brillig, in the slithy toves*
> *Did gyre and gimble in the wabe*
> *All mimsy were the borogroves*
> *And the mome raths outgrabe.*
> *Beware the Iron Men, my son!*
> *The jaws that bite, the teeth that gnash! . . .*

With apologies to Lewis Carroll!

AFTERWORD

The Colorado Mountain Club (CMC), founded in 1912, is pleased to endorse this publication, which complements the club's purpose and mission: "To unite the energy, interest and knowledge of students, explorers and lovers of the mountains of Colorado." The CMC is organized into 15 chapters with 7,000 members throughout the state. Members conduct more than 1,800 events annually in Colorado and other areas of the United States as well as overseas. These events include hiking, backpacking, technical climbing, skiing, snowshoeing, canoeing and rafting, horse and bicycle trips, and trail building. The CMC offers many instructional courses and is a leading organization in conservation and environmental matters. Prospective members are encouraged to learn more about the club by contacting the CMC State Office at 2530 West Alameda Avenue, Denver, CO 80219, telephone (303) 922-8315.

THE PEAKS

The following table correlates the peaks in this book with their altitudes, nearest trailhead and elevation gain from the nearest trailhead. The elevation gains are computed via one of the routes in this book, but the difficulty of the route is ignored. Only the elevation gain required to reach the summit is given. Any elevation gain required on the descent is ignored.

Peak Name	Altitude	Nearest Trailhead	Gain
Andrews Peak	12,565'	East Inlet	4,165'
Arrowhead	12,640+'	Glacier Gorge	3,400'
Baker Mountain	12,397'	Bowen/Baker	3,547'
Bowen Mountain	12,524'	Bowen/Baker	3,674'
Chief Cheley Peak	12,804'	Milner Pass	2,576'
Chiefs Head Peak	13,579'	Glacier Gorge	4,339'
Cleaver	12,200+'	Wild Basin	3,720'
Cracktop	12,760+'	Milner Pass	2,726'
Eagles Beak	12,200'	Wild Basin	3,720'
Elk Tooth	12,848'	Middle Saint Vrain	4,098'
Fairchild Mountain	13,502'	Lawn Lake	4,972'
Farview Mountain	12,246'	Bowen/Baker	3,396'
Flattop Mountain	12,324'	Bear Lake	2,874'
"Fleur de Lis"	12,250'	East Inlet	3,850'
Hagues Peak	13,560'	Lawn Lake	5,030'
Hallett Peak	12,713'	Bear Lake	3,263'
Hayden Spire	12,480+'	Forest Canyon	2,880'

Peak Name	Altitude	Nearest Trailhead	Gain
Howard Mountain	12,810'	Colorado River	3,770'
Isolation Peak	13,118'	Wild Basin	4,638'
Lead Mountain	12,537'	Colorado River	3,497'
Little Matterhorn	11,586'	Bear Lake	2,350'
Longs Peak	14,255'	Longs Peak	4,855'
Lulu Mountain	12,228'	Michigan Lakes	2,448'
McHenrys Peak	13,327'	Glacier Gorge	4,087'
Mount Alice	13,310'	Wild Basin	4,830'
Mount Chiquita	13,069'	Chapin Pass	2,049'
Mount Cirrus	12,797'	Colorado River	3,757'
Mount Copeland	13,176'	Wild Basin	4,696'
Mount Craig	12,007'	East Inlet	3,607'
Mount Cumulus	12,725'	Colorado River	3,685'
Mount Ida	12,880+'	Milner Pass	2,122'
Mount Julian	12,928'	Forest Canyon	3,386'
Mount Lady Washington	13,281'	Longs Peak	3,881'
Mount Meeker	13,911'	Longs Peak	4,511'
Mount Neota	11,734'	La Poudre Pass	1,159'
Mount Nimbus	12,706'	Bowen/Baker	3,856'
Mount Richthofen	12,940'	Lake Agnes	2,690'
Mount Stratus	12,520+'	Bowen/Baker	3,610'
Mummy Mountain	13,425'	Lawn Lake	4,895'
Nakai Peak	12,216'	Green Mountain	3,416'
Nokhu Crags	12,485'	Lake Agnes	2,235'
Notchtop Mountain	12,129'	Bear Lake	2,679'
Ogalalla Peak	13,138'	Middle Saint Vrain	4,388'

Peak Name	Altitude	Nearest Trailhead	Gain
"Ooh La La!"	12,945'	Middle Saint Vrain	4,195'
Otis Peak	12,486'	Bear Lake	3,036'
Ouzel Peak	12,716'	Wild Basin	4,236'
Pagoda Mountain	13,497'	Glacier Gorge	4,257'
Parika Peak	12,394'	Bowen/Baker	3,544'
Pilot Mountain	12,200+'	Wild Basin	3,720'
Powell Peak	13,208'	Glacier Gorge	3,968'
Ptarmigan Mountain	12,324'	East Inlet	3,924'
Ptarmigan Point	12,363'	Bear Lake	2,913'
"Ptarmigans Beak"	12,241'	East Inlet	3,841'
Sharkstooth	12,630+'	Glacier Gorge	3,398'
Snowdrift Peak	12,274'	Green Mountain	3,474'
Spearhead	12,575'	Glacier Gorge	3,335'
Sprague Mountain	12,713'	Green Mountain	3,913'
Static Peak	12,560+'	Lake Agnes	2,310'
Stones Peak	12,922'	Fern Lake	5,008'
Storm Peak	13,326'	Longs Peak	3,926'
Tanima Peak	12,420'	Wild Basin	3,940'
Taylor Peak	13,153'	Glacier Gorge	3,913'
Tepee Mountain	12,360+'	Lake Agnes	2,110'
Terra Tomah Mountain	12,718'	Forest Canyon	2,918'
Thatchtop	12,668'	Glacier Gorge	3,428'
Thunder Mountain	12,040+'	La Poudre Pass	1,865'
Ypsilon Mountain	13,514'	Chapin Pass	2,494'

* CLASSIC ROUTES *

Andrews Glacier of Otis Peak
   II, Class 2, Easy Snow
Chaotic Glacier of Otis Peak
   II, Class 2, Moderate Snow
Chiefs Head-Pagoda Couloir of Chiefs Head Peak
   II, Class 2, Steep Snow
Cracktop Couloir of Cracktop
   III, Class 3, Steep Snow
Dream Weaver of Mount Meeker
   III, Class 4–5.6, Steep Snow/Ice
East Face of Eagles Beak
   II, Class 4
East Face of Nakai Peak
   II, Class 3
East Gully of Sharkstooth
   II, Class 5.4
East Ridge of Ogalalla Peak
   II, Class 4
East Ridge of Ptarmigan Mountain
   II, Class 3
Grand Slam of Longs Peak
   III, Class 3
Hourglass Ridge of Mount Alice
   II, Class 3
Keyhole of Longs Peak
   II, Class 3, (Moderate Snow)
Kieners of Longs Peak
   III, Class 5.0–5.4, ModerateSnow/Ice

Loft of Longs Peak
  II, Class 3, (Moderate Snow)
North Face Couloirs of Flattop Mountain
  I, Class 2, Steep Snow
North Face of Powell Peak
  II, Class 2, Moderate/SteepSnow/Ice
North Ridge of Spearhead
  III, Class 5.6
Northeast Ridge of Sharkstooth
  II, Class 5.6
Notch Couloir of Longs Peak
  III, Class 5.0–5.2, SteepSnow/Ice
Ooh La La Express of "Ooh La La!"
  II, Class 3, Steep Snow
Pfiffner Traverse of the Continental Divide
  (one to two weeks)
Ptarmigan Glacier of Ptarmigan Point
  I, Class 2, Easy/Moderate Snow
Southeast Couloir of Andrews Peak
  II, Class 3, Moderate Snow
Southeast Face and Northeast Ridge of Hayden Spire
  II, Class 5.0–5.2
Spiral Route of Notchtop Mountain
  II, Class 5.4
Stone Man Pass of McHenrys Peak
  II, Class 3
Taylor Glacier of Taylor Peak
  II, Class 3, Steep Snow/Ice
Terra Tomah Mountain-Nakai Peak Divide Traverse
  II, Class 3

Tyndall Glacier of Hallett Peak
  II, Class 2, Moderate/Steep Snow
West Ridge of Isolation Peak
  II, Class 4
Y Couloir of Ypsilon Mountain
  III, Class 5.3–5.4, Steep Snow

INDEX

This index uses the following conventions:

Moderate has been abbreviated to Mod.

The words *in June* or *in Early Summer* have been dropped from some snow ratings. For example, Moderate Snow in Early Summer has been abbreviated to Mod. Snow.

Gerry Roach on Mount Ida on day 16 of the Pfiffner Traverse. August 16, 1987.

ABOUT THE AUTHOR

Gerry Roach is a world-class mountaineer and long-time resident of Boulder, Colorado. After climbing Mount Everest, he went on to become the second person to climb the highest peak on each of the seven continents. In more than 30 years of mountaineering, Gerry has climbed in dozens of states and countries. He has been on more than 20 Alaskan, Andean, and Himalayan expeditions. He is a member of the American Alpine Club.

Closer to home, Gerry has climbed more than 1,000 named peaks in Colorado, including all the fourteeners. He has climbed every named peak in the Colorado counties of Boulder, Gilpin, Clear Creek and Jefferson. He finished climbing every named peak in the Indian Peaks Wilderness and Rocky Mountain National Park in 1978. Gerry is also an accomplished rock climber. His earlier book, *Flatiron Classics*, is a guide to the trails and easier rock climbs in the Flatirons above Boulder.

In *Rocky Mountain National Park*, Gerry conveys his intimate knowledge of Colorado's high peaks. He climbed his first Colorado peak in 1956 and continues to climb actively, returning to the Colorado mountains time and time again to hone his skills. Mountaineering in this rugged and beautiful state forms the foundation for Gerry's successful expeditions to the great peaks of the world.

NOTES

NOTES